TRIGGER WARNING

This book deals with experiences in childhood and adolescent trauma, including addictions, neglect, sexual abuse, incest, physical abuse, and psychological abuse.

DEDICATION

This book is dedicated to my little girl, daughter, son, and future grandbabies. I hope that your lives will be filled with hope, laughter, and love.

To my little girl, deep inside, I hope we can find peace, forgiveness, and our genuine authenticity. I hope we learn how to love and trust profoundly and passionately.

To my daughter and son, thank you for pushing me to follow my dream of writing this book. Your support and love have been the backbone of my healing.

To my future grandbabies, I hope your worlds are full of loving and caring attachments. My dream for you is that we all leave this world a little bit better for you to grow up in.

WHY AM I SPEAKING OUT NOW?

I was a victim. I was abused by my father, stepfather, and other boys/men in my life. I regret not reporting them to the police. I remained silent much of the time. They have most likely gone on to assault other girls/women. I think that it was my fault because I kept quiet. These feelings are prevalent among people who have been abused. I know that when I found the courage to speak up – the people around me who were supposed to protect me did nothing – close family members and supposed friends, along with other government agencies (Child Protection Services), school staff, hospital staff, lawyers, etc. Some of these people witnessed the abuse and ignored it. Seeing them ignore it and look the other way has affected me. It affected me by making me feel like I was unimportant, insignificant, and did not matter. Because they ignored my abuse, it reiterated to me that I could not trust people and that nobody cared. That no one was going to protect me.

I am my only protector. I have assumed for many years that I was the only one who could protect myself. I would not or could not be vulnerable. I have surrounded myself with an impenetrable wall. A huge and thick imaginary barrier that keeps me safe, or so I think. This wall that I thought was protecting me needs to come down. It has caused me additional pain and suffering. It has disabled me to live and love wholeheartedly. I will not let anyone in. I feel I have not been experiencing my true feelings. I cannot cry. I cannot show weakness. I cannot trust people. I cannot be vulnerable with my husband/ life partner. Up until now, this has given power to my abusers—46 years of power.

I am a survivor. As I write this book, many old feelings and memories are bubbling to the surface. I have contacted a therapist to accompany me on my journey. My main goal is to acknowledge the abuse, move through it, and then let it go. I have realized that I will not get this from the actual abusers. They cannot fix it. They have shown me what I do not want in my life. I need to take my power back and let my true soul free. I need to learn to trust others, share intimacy, love unconditionally, access and feel my true feelings.

I am human. We are all humans. We all make mistakes. We all struggle internally. Through this journey of opening up about my past trauma, others and I must remember that the people in my story are all human. Through their individual life journeys – their experiences have made them who they are. It is through their learnt behaviours that my abusers became abusive, and the non-protectors did not protect us. I believe that some people did not have the opportunity to learn new skills or have a break-through to another dimension of thinking when it comes to their own trauma. I hope my story helps others who have been abused or are abusers see they are not alone and that we are only one in many who have endured the abuse and trauma.

This is a recollection of my memories and own experience from my point of view.

I need to figure out where to begin the healing. I think if I start at the beginning...

CHAPTER ONE - THE BEGINNING YEARS

MY STORY BEGINS WITH MY birth in the scenic city of Niagara Falls, in Ontario, Canada. The year was 1978, and I came into this world during the delightful transition from spring to summer when nature was alive with vibrant colours and new beginnings. My mother and father were young and inexperienced. They had no inkling of how to be parents. They had not experienced healthy relationships or upbringings. Both had complicated family histories. Both were born into families with prolonged historical abuse. In a span of the next three years, my two little sisters were born, making our family complete.

I have been told that my parents lived together for a brief time. I do not remember much of my early baby years. I have seen pictures, though. I was a charming little girl with curly blond hair. Looking back at the old photographs, I saw the pure innocence that radiated from me. Although distant, I have some vivid memories of this initial period of innocence. My earliest memory is sitting in a field under a large tree playing. Tiny ants started to crawl on my legs. I recall having the heebie-jeebies and brushing the ants off with urgency. Another time I remember, I was outside playing when I suddenly noticed a bumblebee buzzing around me. Startled, I quickly made my way to the front door and then hurried through the entirety of the house to reach the safety of the back door, hoping to escape the persistent insect. I believe both memories were when my parents and I resided in the house on Crysler Avenue. My father spoke to me about this house in later years. It was a house he purchased. He used to blame my mother for losing it.

I have a faint recollection of a distressing incident. I remember being in a bedroom with my sisters while our parents argued. It was evident that my father was mistreating my mother. We were not allowed to leave the room. I recall feeling terrified for her safety as the argument escalated, with both shouting and the sound of things being thrown around.

After they separated, we moved into a home across the street from my maternal grandmother's house. My mother told me that I was a true escape artist. She said that she had to have many locks on our doors. I would take a chair over and unlock them all. Later in life, I experienced this with my son (my little escape artist). I used to take my middle sibling by her hand on grand adventures to my maternal grandmother's house for tea and toast.

I have a few memories of my mother intoxicated early in my life. My maternal family had a history of alcoholism. I remember an incident when we were at a water fountain in downtown Niagara Falls (Rosberg Family Park). My sisters and I played in the fountain and walked along the cement edge. I think we were waiting for my mother to return from somewhere. We might have been visiting with my father. My mother arrived to take us home. She staggered back from the park. Her unsteady gait made it clear that she was too intoxicated to make it home on her own. She stumbled multiple times, and I was there to help her back on her feet each time. Even at the early age of 3 to 4 years old, I felt a deep concern for her well-being and was determined to ensure she made it home safely.

On another occasion, I had gone to my first sleepover at another girl's house. I was super excited about this. I was watching a movie with her when my aunt called. She said I was needed at home. My aunt came and picked me up from my friend's house. I remember my mother was passed out in her bed. My aunt told me that my sisters wanted me there. I sat at the table with my sisters, and we ate cookies. I have feelings of disappointment attached to this memory.

My maternal family was having a party. I remember being in a bedroom upstairs. I probably was supposed to be asleep. I could hear the laughter and music coming from the lower floor. My uncle came upstairs to retire for the night. He lied down on the bed. He was ready to go to sleep, but I was excited because it meant we would have the chance to play together. I recall jumping up and down on the bed and then lying down quickly to listen to his stomach make gurgling sounds. I found this extremely fascinating. I am not sure which uncle it was. I am sure I was annoying him. My maternal uncles and aunts were teenagers when we were born. I do not have many memories of them in my early life. I remember they would build forts, wrestle, and have epic pillow fights with us.

The day we were removed from my mother, I was five years old. This memory is vivid. I remember we were at a local pub when we ran into one of her ex-boyfriends. Back then, adults could bring their children into pubs and bars. My mother and this ex-boyfriend spoke to each other, and then he left the bar. I recall that she was upset and crying. She told me to tell him she wanted him back or still loved him. I left my mother and sisters at the table and ran after him. I cannot remember what he said to me. But when I returned to the pub, my two little sisters were crying at the table. My mother was passed out. I remember

3

the bartender or server bringing us Shirley Temples. My father showed up at the pub. Someone must have called him. I remember him attempting to shake my mother to wake her up. She would not get up. He could not wake her.

The authorities arrived. I still vividly recall when they took me into one vehicle while my little sisters were ushered into another. The sense of being pulled apart from each other and from my mother left us all in tears... And then, this memory goes black.

I have since forgiven my mother. She was young when she had us, and she also had her own experiences of trauma. She is a significant part of my life presently. I understand that mistakes are a vital part of living. What we do with our mistakes shapes who we will become.

THE LITTLE THINGS

A fresh blank page that has not been written on,
An unborn child's first kick.

Small ripples through a still pond,
The only sound of a clock tick.

The first time making your way through a maze,
The anticipation of a first kiss.

A baby fawn, as you are watching it graze,
The calm that's brought by the winds hiss.

A little boy's first home run,
A hug, when in pain, from your mom.

The feeling of the heat from the hot sun,
The slow rumbling sound of the ocean's hum.

Feeling alone, and the phone rings.
Someone special takes your hand.

All of these are the little things,
That can make life feel so special and grand.

Written on April 23, 1997

CHAPTER TWO - STRANGERS

FAST FORWARD TO US BEING placed in different foster homes for a period. I wouldn't say I liked the foster home I was put in. To the foster family's credit, it probably was not as bad as I remembered because I was so upset then. I had just been ripped away from my mother and had lost my sisters. My whole little world would have been in shambles. My sisters were moved to be with me a while later. I was delighted that we were reunited. I have a few memories of my time with the foster family.

I would start and complete my Kindergarten year with these strangers. I walked to school with their natural children. They had a boy and a girl. My school was a couple of blocks away from their home. Their home was located somewhere on Highland Avenue in Niagara Falls. Their son was very mean to me and would tease me. I was not very nice to him as well. He would purposely get me in trouble. When we walked to school, I would get sick of his antics and run ahead. He attempted to boss me around, but I would not let him. He did not know who I was.

Walking to school with my foster brother, I remembered a building on the corner of Highland Avenue and Lundy's Lane. I passed it on the way to and from school. One of the outer walls had a hole. I believed that the Easter Bunny or other magical creature lived down there. I would envision the magical creature coming out at night, sneaking back, and sleeping during the day. I wonder if it was a family of mystical creatures. For some reason, this building stuck with me even after I grew up. Because later on in my life, as a teenager, I walked by that building. It was like walking down memory lane. It reminded me of my innocence when I was in kindergarten.

The foster home was a two-storey brick house with a big yard. These old brick homes were typical in Niagara Falls. I remember being in trouble and punished for something I had done. I cannot remember what it was. I was told to stay in the bedroom for a time out, isolated from the rest of the kids. I sat by the window, gazing at the other children playing in the backyard. I longed to join them but still felt angry because I was not allowed to do so.

My foster mother would make this concoction of hot potato soup, which she seasoned with too much pepper. I was very vocal about how disgusting it tasted. I had to sit at the kitchen table for a long while and could not eat or finish that soup. I would sneak over to the kitchen garbage and dump it when my foster mother was not in the room.

My little sister used to have temper fits – she would bang her head against the living room floor and scream at the top of her lungs. My foster parents would appear to be upset or worried about my younger sister. I wonder if they knew that we had been neglected and not cared for like we should have been in our baby and toddler years. Our communication skills to get attention or what we wanted was learned behaviours. We had already experienced many broken attachments.

These are the few memories I have of my Kindergarten year. When it was time to leave them, they gave us a mini bible each. I cherished that bible for years afterwards. I also revisited the

foster family later in my teenage years as I had become classmates with their daughter. They seemed nice enough. I do not
have the bible anymore, as it was one of the items lost at my
father's home.

While we spent our time with the foster family, my father and
grandmother went to court and got custody of us. They came to
take us home. I would spend the next 11 years living with them...
the family secrets and sheer horror to come.

The irony is that my chosen career fosters and cares for youth
who can no longer live with their natural families. This experience gave me insight into how it felt to live with strangers, and
because of it, I can better help the youth I care for. Broken attachment is detrimental to humans. We do not want to live with families that are not actually ours. We will create false attachments to
our natural families, believing that they are better than they are.
I have done a lot of work around my broken attachment and still
have a lot of work to do.

GUARDIAN ANGEL

Peering over the clouds, beyond your mortal sight,
I watch over you through the day and darkest night.
Guiding as you tread life's bumpy, winding road,
Ensuring every step propels you toward your destined abode.

Invisible to your eyes, inaudible to your ear,
Yet, if you hold belief, my whispers you will hear.
Mortal form I lack, a human touch denied,
Yet, through your trials, always close by your side.

No miracles I grant, no burdens do I bear,
But in your heart, my presence lingers, always there.
Amidst betrayal, anguish, and moments of dismay,
Rest assured, dear one, in your heart, I forever stay.

Though distant I may seem, a shadow in the night,
Yet truth be told, I stand beside you guiding your sight.
Bound to you with a promise, a vow that's forever true,
Every step you take, the unwavering aid I shall promise to you.

Written on February 07, 1997

CHAPTER THREE - SPIDERS NEST

OUR NEW HOME WAS NESTLED on Dorchester Road. It was a 3-bedroom house with a spacious basement. The yard boasted a generous size, and a large garage stood at the back of the property. My father dedicated countless hours to his passion for rebuilding and working on vehicles. He was, indeed, a jack of all trades, capable of fixing or building just about anything.

My Grandmother was a dedicated Grade One teacher known for her reliability and integrity. Her warm embrace, coupled with her curly, dark hair and hearty figure, made her a comforting presence in those early years. Her culinary skills were second to none; she always prepared meals from scratch. Hailing from Italy, my paternal family heritage heavily influenced her cooking, resulting in some of the most delicious dishes I have ever tasted.

I was six years old when my father and grandmother brought us home. Joy and excitement overwhelmed me as I was out of the stranger's house and now surrounded by my loving family. My father's custody of us was mainly due to my grandmother's influence.

My initial thoughts and feelings quickly changed after we moved in with them. This was not going to be my safe place. I would be lucky to survive the chaos of living under this roof. I would live in constant fear of what would come next. My father was my first abuser – emotionally, physically, and sexually. You never knew the type of man you would receive. Would he be the kind man...would he be the angry man...or would he be the monster...

My sisters and I shared the same bedroom. I remember an imaginary game that we three (my sisters and I) would play at bedtime. We would take turns pretending to be my father. One of us would make the sound effects of him stomping down the stairs and opening our bedroom door. In a deep voice, I would yell and mimic him, "Stop being bad and get to bed now!" "If you girls are good, I will take you to (I would insert a place we really wanted to visit), or you will receive (I would name a treat we liked or gift we wanted.)." My turn would end with making the sound effects of him slamming the door and stomping back up the stairs. We would giggle together, and the next sister would go.

We often played this game while snuggled in the comfort of our beds. I think we played this game to alleviate the worry and distract ourselves from the looming fear of when he would come to our bedroom at night. He would often scold us, find fault with our actions, or enforce punishments that saw us dragged out of our beds in the middle of the night. It did not matter if it was a school day the next morning. At times, it was to redo a chore that he found had not been completed properly. Other times, it was because he was not finished being angry at us for something that occurred earlier in the day. And I think sometimes it was just because he could.

I recall one night at midnight when he woke us up to help him shovel the snow on the driveway. I had something important happening at school the next day. I was exhausted and did not want to help, but I would not dare share those feelings. Sometimes, he would come into the room and not leave. These were the worst times.

A memory I have was when I was in Grade 3 or 4. I awoke one morning to a blood-soaked pyjama shirt, and my underwear bottoms were off. I found them beside the bed. My father brought me to the hospital. On the way there, he repeatedly told me that a young man had assaulted me. He explained that I had to tell the hospital about this when we arrived. I told the hospital attendants precisely what he told me. I was sitting in the hospital room while they spoke to my father outside of the room. I do not know what they talked about. I remember nurses and doctors coming in and out of the room. I received three stitches on the left side of my chest.

On the way home from the hospital and in the days that followed, he kept repeating that a spider had laid eggs in my chest. He said the doctors at the hospital removed it, and that was why I had stitches. As an adult, I have realized this was impossible. A spider cannot lay eggs under your skin. I was confused by what he told me.

I do remember that my father came into my bedroom the night before. He told me I was his favourite. He had a knife. I do not remember what exactly occurred. I blocked this memory out. I do not think that I will ever actually remember the details. I think it is locked in a vault deep in the recesses of my mind. I have since researched how to obtain my medical records from Niagara General Hospital, but I live in another province now. It has proven to be complicated.

I still have a scar on my left breast. I used to have a strawberry birthmark there.

It might not make sense for some people reading about this who have not experienced it. However, many sexual abuse survivors cannot remember the details or events taking place as they have blocked them out. Many go on to experience a lapse of time and memories in their adult experiences with sex. When I read this chapter to my husband, he did not understand how I could not remember. He said that it confused him how, on the one hand, I could remember, and on the other hand, I could not. This is a very regular occurrence for children and victims who have endured abuse.

Throughout my life, I have questioned what is expected regarding love as I was not shown it or did not experience it growing up. Many sexual abuse survivors battle with the thoughts of if they enjoyed it. They were so tiny and innocent that they did not know it was wrong.

MY OWN

Chills run up and down my veins,
Sending into my soul sharp pains.
When a needle pricks such soft skin,
Reminds me of my family's sin.
The hurt that one man caused,
Unto me, taught me not to trust.
The man, my father, talked only of love,
But produced hatred and sin alone.
The only choice left to me.
was to pack my belongings and flee.
This sent me into a land of unfound freedom.
Where I took control and began again.
Freedom, which turned to pure sin.
My soul was lost, and my mind a blur.
Finally, I have found myself again and
developed a life which I love. MY OWN.

Written March 05, 1997

CHAPTER FOUR – GREEN HORNED MONSTER

MY LITTLE SISTER (IN HER adult years) shared a memory with me. She was about four years old, and I would have been six. The adult version of her went to see a Hypnotherapist. During her sessions, she viewed visions (like a movie of her life playing back). She could pause, rewind, or fast-forward these memories. She remembered the green-horned monster coming into her bedroom at night.

When we first moved in with my father, we had a bedroom set up in the basement. It was located next to what my father used as a rec room. His bedroom was located upstairs. My sisters had a bunk bed, and I had a single bed. They were set up beside each other.

Her therapy revealed her memories. The green-horned monster was shown to be my father. She remembered being asleep on the bottom bunk. She vividly recalled that he had come into our bedroom. He pulled off her pyjama bottoms. He touched her in inappropriate ways. After the abuse had occurred, she remembered me coming into her bed and helping her pull up her pyjama bottoms. My middle sister stuck her head over from the top bunk to see if she was okay. I reassured them both that it would be all right. (Even though it wasn't, and it would not be.) Her adult version now understood why she feared the dark for most of her life and could only sleep in a position with a view of the door.

This jogged a memory deep down inside me. This was a point in time when my little sister would wake up screaming in the morning. She appeared deathly afraid. She was visually upset. My father would state that she must have snuck upstairs in the middle of the night and watched a scary movie on the television. She would bring up the green-horned monster for years afterwards. My father would always resort to making fun of her. He placed the blame on her and told her to get over it. Monsters were not real.

Some were little memories that now had meaning, like when he would have the three of us pull down our bathing suits while swimming in our backyard pool and stand looming over us, staring. There is an uncomfortable feeling attached to this. This was not a choice but forced. He used to say that we were doing it to help my middle sister so that she could tan her burns (more on this in the next chapter).

We all remember him calling us into his bed on multiple occasions. I believe that he had us touch him inappropriately and forced us to suck his penis. He would tell each of us that we were his favourite. He would also say that it was our little secret and not to tell our sisters.

He chased us around the backyard with his penis hanging out, trying to urinate on us. What grown man would do this to his little girls? I remember being terrified and running as fast as I could away from him. I did not want to get urinated on. He was laughing. He thought it was funny. There are feelings of repulsion that are attached to this memory.

I remember other sporadic nightly visits. I have memories of him coming into our bedroom. Something terrible did happen during these visits, but I cannot recall precisely what it was. These visits stopped when I was in Grade 6. This is when I hit puberty. My breasts started growing. I remember I asked him his opinion on whether my bra was appropriately fitted. He immediately became angry and told me not to show him. He told me to ask my grandmother. I was confused. I remember feeling that this was off-putting and out of his norm.

Also, I remember being jealous of the attention my step-mother received when she came into the picture. I believe this was around when I was in Grade 5 or 6. I did not like her because I felt that she had stolen my father from me. I mention this because I am unsure if it had to do with the sexual abuse abruptly stopping.

Around this time, I would punish myself in bed at night. I would put myself in uncomfortable positions for lengthy periods and then attempt to sleep like that. I would pinch and hit myself. I remember wanting to be in pain because I thought I deserved it. I told myself that I had been bad. I do not know what it was that I had done that was so bad.

I believe that due to the repeated sexual assaults from my father, I mimicked him when I was little. I was a little kid abusing other little kids. I would inappropriately touch my cousins, little sisters, and elementary school peers. I would have constant inappropriate thoughts about the neighbour boy. I realized what I had been doing was wrong when I started my Grade 7 school year. I do not know how I came upon the knowledge. It could have been in health class, or I realized it with some maturity. I felt very dirty and shameful. This feeling followed me throughout my teenage and early adult life. I apologized to the ones that I had victimized. I explained that I had been wrong and felt terrible.

Many abuse survivors go on to be abusers themselves. I was fortunate that my little mind realized when it did. Not many survivors get that opportunity. My father and stepfather had taught me this behaviour—more about my stepfather's abuse in later chapters. I mimicked the two people who had been my only male role models. I grew up with sexual abuse from men who were supposed to be my fathers. I did not think it was strange that my father abused me. I felt that this was a normal thing in all families.

STORMY DAY

It's raining outside, dark, and cold,
As I contemplate the story about to unfold.
The fury of your storm unleashed onto me,
It leaves me grappling with the challenge to see.
Everything I cherish slips through my hand,
Like your toes on the beach drifting through sand.
As you gaze into my teary, red eyes,
I hope you grasp the agony caused by your lies.
Do you see the wreckage your abuse has sown,
Leaving me to grapple with my innocence being thrown.
I felt my control being ripped away,
As I was left with the anguish of what happened today.
When will my doubts and fears start to relent,
Will the ache I feel dissolve like the wind's lament?
Will I have forgotten when the storm finally clears,
When the birds start to sing, and the sun reappears.

Written on March 09, 1997

CHAPTER FIVE – HOT WATER

ON MANY OCCASIONS, MY FATHER would chase us when we were naked. I have memories of being terrified. I remember hiding behind my grandmother's chair in the living room. My grandmother did nothing to stop him.

Once he caught me, he would drag me to the bathroom. He had filled the tub up with only hot water. He punished me by making me stand in a tub of hot water. He would force us into the tub. I remember him telling us to dance. He enjoyed watching us. I had to stand in the tub, which was impossible as the water temperature was too hot. I would sort of dance in an attempt not to let my skin touch the water. When I got out, my feet would be very red. This was one of my father's early "go-to" punishments.

One day, we came home from school. He had a friend over. He found a lunch thrown away in the backyard garbage can. He asked us (his three little girls) whose sandwich it was. I was in Grade three, my middle sister was in Grade one, and my baby sister was in kindergarten. All I knew was that it was not mine. I told him so. No one would admit to it being their lunch—rightfully so, as we knew what would come next. In later years, my youngest sister admitted it was hers.

My father sent my youngest sister into the living room. He went on to question my middle sister and me. When my father raged – his eyes would bulge out. He had huge eyes. He was angry, and his eyes were bulging out. He started the bathtub and told us we would both be punished if someone did not admit it. My middle sister and I were crying and screaming. We were terrified. He grabbed me and dragged me towards the bathroom. He was about to throw me in when my middle sister took the blame. I remember him chasing her into our bedroom. She attempted to hide. I remember her crying and stating that she did not do it. He was dragging her towards the bathroom. She was resisting just like I had. He sent my little sister and me outside. His friend was still outside.

Shortly after, my father came outside and told his friend to leave. He did. He asked my little sister and I to go into the house with him. My middle sister was in the bathroom, crying and crouched on the toilet. She did not say anything. We did not dare say anything. We were crying. I could see that her skin was peeling off her body. She was hurt badly. She needed to go to the hospital. He was not taking her.

He forced us to peel off the dead skin that was hanging. He repeatedly stated that this is what happens to you when you are bad, and that God was punishing her. Why was he not taking her to the hospital? My grandmother was not home. We were in shock. He did this to her. I felt guilty. I should have taken the blame. I was the eldest. I should have protected her and just let him throw me in. I carried that guilt around for a long time.

Once my grandmother came home – he kept repeating to her that my sister had fallen into the tub. It was an accident. My grandmother told him to take her to the hospital. On the way to the hospital – he repeatedly told my middle sister that she fell into the tub. She was in shock. She did not speak. She would not talk, laugh, or show emotions for seven months after the incident. My father would spend that time convincing himself and us that she fell in, that it was an accident, and blame my paternal grandfather for turning the temperature up on the furnace too high. Still, to this day, he has not taken responsibility for it. Still, to this day, my sister must wear the scars. Scars that cover 65% of her body.

My mother did not know this had happened. For six months, while my sister was in the hospital, my father lied to my mother. He made excuses of why she could not have us for a visit. Finally, he had to tell her that there was an accident, and my middle sister was in the hospital. My mother and stepfather went to visit her in the hospital. My sister told her what had happened. She told her that my father had lied and had thrown her into a tub of hot water. She finally spoke and was able to release her tears. My mother and she cried together. My mother found a nurse and told her.

I want to reiterate that this was over a sandwich being thrown out.

My middle sister and I are very close now. We work together, helping other children and youth in the foster care system. Our experiences have made us who we are. She is a powerful, independent woman. She had to endure bullying from her peers at school. They would belittle her and call her names. She has endured stranger's stares—strangers who do not know what happened to her, strangers who assumed she might have a disease or did something wrong herself. She is the most tenacious woman I know, and I have nothing but mad respect for her.

I do not notice her burn scars anymore. I see past that. I notice, occasionally, the looks and stares that she receives. She has this grace about her—a knowledge that some people are ignorant of. She cares with all her might and being. She has an empathy that cannot be matched. I absolutely adore her. She is a true testament to what a survivor is.

BODY, HEART, AND SOUL

The rage runs through my veins uncontained,
As if someone has pierced my heart with pain.
Feelings of madness and hurt collide,
Love and hate within me fiercely vie.

My soul feels like it has been crumpled up,
My body feels as if it's been ripped apart.
My head thumps with a relentless beat,
Love morphs to hate, and joy to defeat.

Love seems to have abandoned my whole being,
Happiness tangled in knots, the hurt unyielding.
Thoughts crush me like a weight so vast,
Feelings inside me provoke extreme contrast.

The past confronts me, stirring profound reactions,
Does his body, heart, and soul face similar fractions?
I wonder if the hurt echoes within his core,
As much as in mine, does it leave him sore?

Written March 09, 1997

CHAPTER SIX – THE COVER UP

THE PERIOD AFTER IT WAS revealed that our father caused my sister's burns is a blur. My father went to great lengths to keep the truth a secret, and my mother went to great lengths to attempt to save us. At first, we would visit my sister in the hospital. But when the truth came out, my father enforced a rule that nobody was allowed to go – not us and not my paternal family. He also stopped us from seeing my mother.

My middle sister spent time in multiple hospitals over the next year. She was in a coma for six months. The procedures and operations she had to endure were endless. Ice baths, skin grafts, etc. She had two staff in her room to watch over her because she was not expected to live. When she awoke, she would not talk, refused to eat, and could not walk. She remembers ripping out the nose tube that was feeding her. She told me that she would visit the teenage boy across the hall, and he would feed her mini cheeseburgers from McDonald's. It was the only food she would eat. She slept on a sand bed because she could not be in a regular bed. She could not straighten her right arm out (she still cannot). She had to go through extensive Physiotherapy to learn how to walk again. She had to wear a protective covering over her skin and different braces on her arm and leg. She had to wear jobes (pressure garments) for years afterwards.

Before being released, she was transferred to McMaster Children's Hospital's burn unit in Toronto, Ontario. That was where the burn specialist was located. My father and a close friend of his went to visit her. My father kidnapped her from the hospital and took her to an abandoned building somewhere in downtown Toronto. He left his friend at the hospital. He used the time to convince my middle sister to tell everyone that it was an accident so that she would not be taken away from him. He told her to say that my mother had made her say that he had burned her. He told her that she would not see her sisters again if she did not do this. He brought her back to the hospital. The vehicle was surrounded by police officers with guns drawn. They took my father and middle sister back inside the hospital. He was not arrested.

My father had hired a reputable lawyer. My mother was fighting him in court. I remember social workers visiting me at school and home. My father prepared us for the questions. We spent gruelling hours going over what we were to tell them. He threatened us with the fear that they would take us away and we would end up somewhere scary. (Like we were not already in the most terrifying place.) He would tell us that family had to be loyal to each other. We would answer their questions just like our father advised us to. We would be his good little girls. We would not go against the family.

After the hospital, my middle sister was sent to live with a foster family. They allowed my father to see my middle sister at that time. Her abuser. The one who harmed her. He would pick her up from the foster family and bring her to counselling appointments, Physiotherapy, and other medical appointments. During that unsupervised access, he coaxed her into saying that my mother had lied and had bribed her with candy. All with the promise that she could return home to her sisters and family. He won the court case, and she was returned to her abuser. Again, how did they not know? How did the system fail us?

He would never use the hot water punishment with us again. It was rumoured, though, that he had burned one of his girl-friends with the same type of punishment.

He made my middle sister wear long-sleeved clothing throughout the rest of her time living with him. She was not allowed to wear shorts. He would make her wear it even through-out the sweltering summer months. It is my opinion that he did not want to see it himself. He did not want others to see it. To see what he had done to his daughter.

I found the court book from this trial later in my early teenage years. It is in that book that I learned about a disturbing inci-dent in my father's past. His father (my grandfather) was a very abusive man (straight off the boat from Sicily, Italy). His father had caught him smoking cigarettes. He punished my father by tying him to a pole in the basement for three days. My grand-mother would go down and spoon-feed him. But he had to urinate and defecate in a towel. I am aware that my father was abused. He did not break the cycle of abuse.

The Paternal Grandfather I knew; I did not know well. He was not living at the Dorchester house. He would visit, though. He had once hit my little sister with a two-by-four because she broke her bed accidentally by jumping up and down on it. My father shared with me that his father told him multiple times not to go for custody of us because we were not worth it. My father was very manipulative. He brought this comment up a lot throughout my life. I am not sure how much truth there was to it.

My grandmother hinted that my grandfather spent much of his time at the horse track. It was one of his favourite hobbies. She also hinted at what he did to their kids (my father, paternal uncles, and aunt). My grandfather abused my grandmother and her children. I believe that is why she did not get involved when my father abused us – as she had triggers and learnt behaviour.

The court book also revealed that my mother and stepfather put up a good fight for us. My mother tried to get justice for my middle sister while simultaneously trying to protect us. She exhausted every effort that she could. In the end, it did not matter. At least my mother had tried. Others in our life did not.

TRUST AND ANGUISH

The dark realm of nightmares
Ignorance is a mistake.
Overcoming my past requires effort.
But reality always creeps back in
My emotions become entangled.
Leaving me unable to sleep
Self-control disintegrates.
My anguish is partly my fault.
Yet partly blamed on others
Simple solutions seem elusive.
Hatred, disgust, and distrust
None of these are my ways.
They do not bring happiness.
Scared of the outside world
Yet always looking in
Trusting others is not easy.
But it is hard not to give one soul that trust.
Seemingly impossible to overcome.
But experiences change situations.
I am certain of my willpower to succeed.

Written: November 29, 1998

CHAPTER SEVEN – CORE PHYSICAL PUNISHMENTS

MY FATHER HAD AN ARSENAL of punishments he chose to use. He had demons living inside of him that often reared their ugly heads. It is my opinion that when he punished us, it gave him a sense of power that he liked. It was a release for his pent-up emotions. He was often smiling or laughing during his episodes of torment.

"Running up and down the stairs" was a go-to punishment for my father. He often stood at the bottom of the stairs with a belt. Simultaneously, while I ran up and down, I was forced to chant a line, such as "I must respect my elders." At the bottom of the stairs, he would be waiting. He would then whip me with the belt buckle side of the belt. I would cry. He would tell me to stop crying. Sometimes, I would fall. He would then yell at me to get up and go faster. The problem was that I did not want to return to the bottom of the stairs where he was waiting. I remember being out of breath and panting while chanting the line repeatedly. My tears were pouring down my face! I was hot. My fear was in my throat. I felt like I was going to vomit. But I would not dare stop. It would continue until he told me that I could stop. Sometimes, he would not stand at the bottom of the stairs. I felt some relief when he was not there.

After one of these times, I remember attending my elementary school, black and blue. My legs had deep lacerations with dried-up blood. One of my classmates asked me what had happened. This was one of the occasions when I shared my secret. I told him that my father abused me. He shared with me that his father hurt him as well. The teachers and principal never asked what had happened. It was not like they could not see it. They just looked the other way. Physical abuse was very prominent back then and still is. People minded their own business, even if it was a little girl.

He would chase us often. He liked to chase us. Sometimes, it would start as a game, but it frequently turned into horror. Sometimes, when he caught me, he would tickle me until I was crying – begging him to stop. Sometimes, he would hold me down against my will and lick my face. It was torture. Other times, I would be running for my life because when he caught up with me, he would repeatedly kick me or hit me with his hand or weapon (The belt was his weapon of choice). These chases usually ended with him looming over me while I was curled up in the fetal position – crying and begging him to stop. I found myself in this position a lot as a kid.

He would throw us over his lap often. He would hit us with the belt buckle, a stick, or his hand. I would attempt to cover my bottom with my hand. He would tell me not to do that. At times, he would continue and hit my hands. Other times, he would hold my arms at my sides so that I could not protect myself and continue hitting. I cried and begged for him to stop. He did not. After these punishments, I often had welts and bruises on my lower back and bottom.

34

He once duct-taped my entire body. I remember begging him to stop as I felt an overwhelming sense of loss of control. I could not move at all. I was lying there in the middle of the hallway, crying and hyperventilating. He was laughing. He thought it was funny. He left me taped up for an extended time before removing it. I felt a sense of embarrassment. No one helped me. My grandmother was there. She just stood by and watched.

One of his other go-to punishments was to make us "stand or kneel in the corner," facing the wall for hours. We were told not to move, and we dared not. I remember my knees hurting and my body aching from being in the same position for so long. Sometimes, my father would watch a movie with the other girls (who were not being punished) or play a board game. He did this purposely. He was very psychological like that.

There was an old wine cellar in the back corner of the basement. The cellar was about 6 feet by 3 feet. It was a tiny dark room with spider webs and dust. He would grab you, push you in, shut the door, and lock it. It did not matter if I begged him not to or told him I would never do it again. He would not listen. Once in the cellar, the only light visible seeped in through a small hole at the top of the room. He would leave you in there for hours. Nobody would be on the other side. During these types of punishments, I would check out and go numb. I was so afraid. Afraid of being left alone and isolated. Later, into my early adolescence, this cellar was knocked down – no more walls or door. I was pleased and relieved to see it go. I had my own private celebration.

During these abuses, I remember feeling tremendous guilt if I was not the one being punished. Either way, I thought we were all being punished. As the older sister, I felt I should have intercepted and saved my sisters, but I was just a little girl. I was powerless against him.

I was an angry little girl with a lot of pent-up emotions. I was very destructive. I climbed the fence into the back neighbour's yard and smashed their sprinkler into many pieces. I went to the neighbour's house to our right when they were on vacation. I threw all their shoes around in the front entry they had left open. I went to their trailer and destroyed the inside – emptying the cutlery drawer onto the floor, taking things out of the cupboard, and throwing them around. I broke off important pieces outside of the trailer. I had no ill will or reason to do this to our friendly neighbours. I do remember feeling an overwhelming sense of anger. I was so angry with my father but could not express my true feelings to him, so I took it out on the innocent neighbours.

My grandmother was often a witness, and she did nothing. Other family members and my father's friends knew that he was hurting and abusing us and did not help us—these three little girls.

Even as I write this, I cannot describe or tell you how often these abuses occurred. I know it was many. I cannot express the fear I lived in every day of my childhood because I usually checked out. I went numb. I learned to shut the feelings off. I know that nobody helped me. I felt that nobody could. My natural reaction to writing this book has been to stop and not finish the book. I keep thinking this is in the past. There is nothing you can do about it. Stop reliving the feelings; it is a waste of time.

I believe a lot of people who have survived this type of abuse feel this way. It is a protection mechanism built in. A way that we developed to survive it. I still have this superpower—the power to flick the switch, turn off my emotions, and survive.

GO AWAY HURT

Go away, feelings of hurt.
Why can't I get rid of you,
Like I did the people who gave you to me.
Why can't I trust just a few,

Be happy instead of feeling the pain.
Why can't you dissipate,
Go away and never show your face again.
Is this always going to be my fate?

I'll hurl you away just like the rest.
I hate and despise feeling this way.
I am sending you to those who deserve it the most.
And they can have the price to pay.

Go away and never return.
I am begging you to leave me.
I do not want you anymore.
GO AWAY, feelings of hurt, and please set me free.

Written on January 07, 1998

CHAPTER EIGHT – PSYCHOLOGICAL WARFARE

THIS WAS PROBABLY THE HARDEST one of the abuses. Scars usually healed. Healing my mind, on the other hand, has been difficult. My father was very manipulative and controlling. I believe my father had an undiagnosed mental illness. I think he was Bi-polar. He had manic tendencies. He would put us in harm's way on purpose. He was highly paranoid. He often thought that airplanes flying overhead were watching him. He told me once that the neighbour had a camera aimed at our house and was recording us.

Sifting through these memories has been the most brutal and most revealing.

He forced us to watch while he broke all our toys and discarded them into garbage bags. He loaded them into his vehicle and told us to get in. He would drive us around, find a dumpster, and throw the bags into it. I remember being so upset because I had some forever-lost favourites: my Barbie Escapade doll, my calligraphy set, and so much more. He never returned to retrieve our toys, even though I wished he did.

One Christmas, my father had told us that he had shot Santa Claus and that he no longer would come at Christmas. He went as far as not celebrating it that year. He said that we hadn't been good and didn't deserve it. I remember us being adamantly upset. We did not have our traditional Christmas dinner with the family. It was a few weeks later that a few bags of presents ended up on the front step. Maybe he felt some guilt (if he was even capable of that).

He was highly manipulative even during family outings (supposed good memories). My father had a lot of toys: a trike, a sports car, and a boat. He would launch his boat from the ramp in Chippawa, Ontario, and then navigate the waters, heading downstream towards the awe-inspiring Niagara Falls. He would drift past the sign at the top that advised you not to go any further. It had large, bright, red letters reading DANGER and KEEP OUT. I remember yelling at him to take us back to safer waters. He would not. I remember being extremely afraid that the boat would be pulled over the falls and we would all die. He would push the boundary and drive as close as possible to the top of the falls. We could see a structure of some sort under the water stretching across. He did this on multiple occasions.

He would also take us boating to one of the great lakes and Crystal Beach. He attached the different inflatables to the back of the boat. I remember sitting on the boat in fear and anticipating my next turn. It wasn't enough for him that I lay or sit on the inflatable. He would force me to stand on it. I did not have a choice. I remember being scared the entire time that he pulled me. He drove erratically. Needless to say, I did not trust him at all. I could clearly see the bottom of the lake. The rocks looked like they were immediately beneath me. I thought that if I fell, I might crash into those rocks. I found that my father immensely enjoyed it when we were scared. It did something for him. I wouldn't say I liked boating. To this day, I do not choose to boat in my adult life.

My grandmother would cook but did not clean the house. We were my father's little housekeepers. He would force me to clean all the time. The entire house cleaning was our responsibility. Suppose he found a spot I had missed while washing dishes. He would remove the entire cupboard of dishes and make me rewash all of them. I vividly remember scrubbing the kitchen floor on my hands and knees. He came to inspect it. He found a small black scuff mark and told me I had not done it correctly. He said I had to redo the whole kitchen floor again. I remember once mumbling under my breath that I was not Cinderella. He became so angry that he hit and kicked me while I lay in a fetal position. He told me that after I finished redoing the floor, I would have to write ten pages (back and front) of lines. "I must not mouth off to my elders."

I had to do our laundry. If socks were missing because the laundry machine ate them, which it often did, we would get into trouble. He would yell at us and force us to search the house for them. If we did not find them, he would find a punishment that he found just. I remember him waking us in the middle of the night and forcing us to do chores that he felt were not completed correctly.

We did not just have to keep the house spotless; we also had to do the outside chores: washing the driveway, shovelling the snow during the winter, gardening, and weeding, washing his vehicles, scrubbing down the bottom of the boat, and so on. With all the chores and duties came many opportunities not to do it to his standards or mess it up altogether.

He often told me that I was lazy. To this day, I still have a tough time with cleaning. It is triggering. I cannot just surface clean. I must do a more thorough job each time, like moving my furniture and getting underneath, which must be done perfectly.

I often will not do it because it always feels like a more enormous feat than it is. As an adult, I have hired a housekeeper to help me. I have also turned on my music to help me along. I am practicing just surface cleaning. I have recently started gardening again. I am beginning to like it.

He used to make me write pages of lines, including popular phrases such as "I must always respect my elders," "I must not mouth back," and "I must not lie." Writing lines was a punishment my father often used in my later childhood. You could not move from where you sat until you showed him the completed pages. My fingers were usually numb, and my hands ached and cramped after such writing.

I remember an incident where I was recording songs from the radio to my tape cassette in the living room. I sat on the glass living room table and fell through. I had deep cuts on my legs. My father was not home. I anticipated his reaction and worried about the trouble I would get into. When he finally did come home, he immediately became furious and called me stupid. He yelled at me for a while. Who sits on a glass coffee table. He did not take care of my cuts but sent me to the basement to write lines. "I must not sit on a glass table." My grandmother helped with my cuts later.

Sometimes, he forced me to lie because he would not listen to me or accept my truth. My grandmother went on weekend trips to see my aunt, who resided in Toronto. My grandmother accidentally knocked over the sugar bowl on the kitchen table before leaving for her trip to Toronto. She forgot to clean it. My father found it. He asked me if I had done it. I told him adamantly that I had not. He would not accept my answer. He repeatedly hit me until I said I had done it. After I admitted the lie, he dragged me to the bathroom and rubbed my face against the floor behind the toilet. I attempted to escape him, but that only worsened things. I was disgusted. He then advised me to clean the entire bathroom spotless.

Part of our morning routine was to wake my father before leaving for school. If we were unsuccessful, we would get into trouble. Sometimes, he would wake up angry over something that did not legitimately happen. This one time, he thought someone ate a whole pie. There was no pie. I told him he was dreaming. He was adamant that someone had stolen the pie. We had to kneel outside his bedroom door until someone admitted they did it, or he fully awoke and realized he dreamed about it. I missed out on an exciting school trip (the few I was allowed to go on). I was so angry and disappointed. When he got out of bed – he told me I should have fully woken him, and then I would have been able to go. Of course, it was my fault, as always. He would never admit to his wrongdoings.

This was the constant mental state that I lived in, not knowing how he would react or what he could say. At the time, I did not realize that he was not normal. In these last few chapters, I have found myself rushing to escape my father's reality. I do not want to be sucked back in.

My father never got help for his mental health. Our family ignored it. Living with our mentally ill father affected us deeply as three little girls. It exposed us to challenging social and psychological situations. These experiences in our childhood stayed with us into adulthood. They shaped how we saw ourselves and the world.

ARE MY THOUGHTS MINE

I sit and ponder as all seems well.
Then thoughts creep into my head.
Are these thoughts truly mine? I cannot tell.
Some thoughts feel like they've been fed.

Am I wrong for being who I am?
To choose happiness over sorrow,
To be the lion, not the lamb.
What should happen tomorrow?

Am I right to not care so much?
For loving everyone the same,
For giving away my gentle touch,
And sometimes being outright lame.

Is it wrong to hold my needs dear,
To shield my heart from caring too much,
To guard my emotions, never to appear,
Wouldn't you do the same as such?

If your family stole away your rights to be you,
Robbed your mind and snatched your thoughts away!
Wouldn't you question what is true?
Their thoughts or mine, this thought haunts me every day.

Written on November 28, 1997

CHAPTER NINE – HIDDEN AWAY

YOU MIGHT HAVE BEEN WAITING to see what happened to my mother after my first chapter. I have mentioned her a few times. I will catch you up. After losing us, my mother went on a healing journey in Edmonton. She had stopped drinking. Losing us was devasting for her, and she wanted us back. When she felt she was ready, she came back for us. My first memory of seeing her for the first time was at my school. I was in Grade Two at Mary Ward Elementary in Niagara Falls, Ontario. She came to the school with my father. My teacher came to my desk and told me to go with him outside. He walked me out of the portable. There she was, standing with my father. My mother had returned, and I remember feeling elated and happy to see her. This is a memory etched in my mind. She was glowing and radiating. She looked beautiful.

My father hated my mother. He set up a version of my mother that best suited his needs at any given time. He told me that she had ruined his life. He would remind me often that she lost us and that he had saved us. He never had a kind word to say about her. He put her down constantly and called her not-so-nice names.

My father told us stories about how my mother was when we lived with her before he got custody of us. He repeatedly told the same stories, ensuring they were embedded into our minds. He told us that there was no food in her house because she spent all her money on booze. That we always went hungry. He would add that he had to buy us food and diapers and drop them off with her because she could not afford them. He often mentioned that my mother never cleaned the house or did the laundry. He said that when he picked us up for visits, her house frequently had ceiling-high piles of laundry, dirty dishes on the counters, and garbage strewn about. He would add that it was not a healthy environment for us. And again, he would remind us that he had saved us from that.

He felt we were ungrateful about the fact that he had saved us from the situation our mother had us in. He would tell us this when he felt we were being bad little girls and not listening to him. He told me that my mother cheated on him when they were together. He said that she even slept with his best friend. He told me that she had ruined his life and broke his heart. He worked aggressively hard at turning us against her.

He often told me that I reminded him of her, and he shared that this upset him. He stressed that he did not want me to turn out like her. He often said I was acting like her, calling me a liar, lazy, or stupid. He would regularly put me down and add that I was being just like my mother. How often have I heard that line? He used mind games to manipulate and control me.

When I asked my mother about my father's stories, she said it wasn't true. I think she asked him why he would say those hurtful things after we visited with her. He would blame my sisters and me. He would tell my mother that we were causing problems between them and then frequently criticize us for it. He claimed to my mother that we were manipulating them against each other, perhaps to cover up his actions, especially if

46

we had confided in our mother. There were times when we did tell our mother about his abusive behaviour.

This one evening, after one of our first visits with my mother. We were crying because we did not want to leave her. We often missed her when the visit ended. He drove us to a quiet street. We did not know where we were. It was dark outside. He opened the car door. He ordered us to leave and walk to her house. He said that if we wanted to go live with her, we could; we just had to get out of the car and find her home. This, again, was a mind game. My father knew that, as little girls, we would not leave the car, go into the dark, and go out into an unknown place. I wished I had gotten out of the car for many years afterwards. I do not think he would have let me leave, though. He used this time to drive it home; he cared for us, and she did not. I learned quickly not to share too many emotions or thoughts about my mother or our visits. Even though, after each visit, he would grill us for information.

My father would inform me when it was time for my mother to come for a visit. Sometimes, I remember waiting for her, but she did not come. I sat on the front porch or by our living room window, patiently staring and waiting for her vehicle to pull in. I would sit there for hours, anticipating her arrival. I felt extremely sad and disappointed when she did come. I looked forward to the visits with my mother. It was an escape from my reality—or my father's reality.

My father explained to me that this was how my mother was and reiterated that I should not and could not depend on her. He did this on many occasions. I later discovered there was no planned visit. He either made it up, called it off, or disappeared when she came to pick us up. My mother attempted to right this through the courts as she had court-ordered visitation. He had lied to me about the supposed visits on purpose, repeatedly making me experience disappointment and sadness to ensure that I believed the lies he told me about my mother.

We had relocated our bedroom to the main level of the house, and our old bedroom became his living quarters. It was furnished with a living room and his bedroom. He had guns displayed on the living room wall. He had constructed a 12-foot by 12-foot, sturdy, rolling, heavy door with a large padlock. He was the only one with the key. He had also installed a secret exit from his bedroom closet that led to a small area with a built-in toilet.

Sometimes, my father would instruct us to go to the basement and hide in his living space, which we called "the dungeon" but, looking back, should have been called "the fortress." He told us to be quiet and not make a sound. He would roll the heavy door shut and lock us in. My sisters and I were terrified. We always thought that bad people were coming for us. That there was something much bigger going on. Later, I discovered he was hiding us from our mother and the authorities.

My mother would call the police after she arrived at the house to pick us up, and we were not there (or so my father said). The police would come to the house but did not find us. They did not force my father to open the locked door. We did hear mumbling outside the door, but the door never opened. My mother and the police would leave, and my father would come down and tell us it was safe to come out.

I remember a period when we lived out of the family van. It was an older Grey GMC van. It had a queen-sized bed that my father had built in the back. It was similar to a creeper van. To me, a creeper van is a van with blacked out windows that strangers drive and kidnap children with. We felt like we were on an adventure at that early age. We visited many places and slept in different spots - fields, parking lots, and my father's friend's and family's driveways. I remember asking my father when we were going back home. He replied to me when it was safe to do so.

Later, I found out that we were in hiding. Once again, my father kept us from seeing my mother.

Despite my mother's efforts to see us, my father kept us away from her because he enjoyed controlling both her and us. It seemed like he wanted to punish my mother, and he often used her as an excuse for his behaviour. I also believe he was trying to keep his secrets hidden. As I got older, the visits with my mother became more regular. I remember my parents keeping a calendar to ensure the visits were consistent, perhaps because a judge intervened for our benefit.

ME OR MYSELF

I am an unfeeling spirit with no remorse for what I do.
Watch myself soar above, taking me only, not you!
Do not condemn me for your faults, which I myself have not.
I will not accept them, as I need to tend to my own thought.

Watch me go and listen to my voice,
You're the one who fucked up, so you don't have the choice.
I trusted you and gave away my heart.
You lied to me as you did not think of me as smart.

I cared for you, and I do not know what the fuck for.
You lied to me, and I don't trust you anymore.
Watch me go cold, no feelings to show you at all.
You have screwed it up and I will watch you fall.

I am not going to help, there is no second chance.
You will be ignored. I won't give a second glance.
My feelings are locked in a box on my shelf.
Are you confused, then you do not know me or myself?

Written February 14, 1997

CHAPTER TEN - NEW EDITION

AND THIS IS A GREAT time to introduce my stepfather. My mother met my stepfather in Edmonton. They lived together in a small suite when they returned to Niagara Falls. He was studying Computer Programming in Toronto. Initially, he seemed like a wonderful man who cared deeply for my mother. When I was young, he was a stranger, but I grew to like him quickly. However, it would not take long before my feelings towards him changed, and I grew to despise him.

They moved to Ottawa shortly afterwards. He and my mother married at a Justice of the Peace in Ottawa, Ontario, on October 21, 1986. It was a small ceremony with a few of their close friends. I did not attend the ceremony as I was still residing with my father. This would have been approximately two years after my stepfather had entered my life. I was eight years old.

He appeared to make my mother happy. He took care of her. He seemed to want to get to know us girls. When we visited them, we would do fun things together: go on camping trips, visit theme parks, go out to restaurants, and visit our maternal families. We spent quality time together. I got to know and trust him at first. He became my stepfather in my eyes. I was in desperate need of a healthy male role model.

My mother and stepfather wanted a baby. It was a planned pregnancy. They sat the three of us down and told us the news. We were excited for them. My mother underwent IVF (In Vitro Fertilization), which is the process of fertilization where an egg is combined with sperm in vitro. She had had her tubes tied or burned earlier in her life after we three were born. The IVF was successful; my baby brother was born November 02, 1991. He was a beautiful baby boy. He was so tiny. Us girls were over the moon about him. My stepfather and mother appeared delighted. I was 13 when he was born.

My Mother and stepfather had two homes that I remember well – first in Woodbridge, Ontario and then in Tottenham, Ontario. The one in Woodbridge had a vast, wooded area next to it. This is where my sisters and I would roam and play. We built a fort near the house. We were on one of our many adventures when my little sister stepped on a beehive. I remember the swarm of bees surrounding her. I ran so fast into the house and left her behind. She ended up being stung multiple times. My mother helped her and took care of the multiple bee stings. She had calamine lotion all over her body. I remember thinking that she looked hilarious.

I remember having my first real heart-to-heart with my mother about my stepfather in Woodbridge. I had shared my feelings and thoughts with my paternal grandmother (the one I lived with) about how my stepfather made me feel uncomfortable. She had told me to talk to my mother about it. I told my mother that my stepfather made me feel highly uncomfortable. It took a lot of courage. I shared with her that I found him overly touchy and loving. My mother told me that he only cared about me, and this is how he showed his feelings and affection. She said I felt uncomfortable because I was not used to a father figure showing me that love. What she said made sense to me. I explained to her that I did not want him to hug me so often or cuddle me too much. She did speak to my stepfather about it. This seemed to help for a brief time.

We moved my stepfather and mother from Woodbridge to Tottenham. My stepfather and I were driving the moving truck. We had stopped to help a couple on the side of the road. When we returned to the moving truck, I remember him repeatedly telling me how strange it was that they thought we were a couple. I found the conversation uncomfortable and unnerving. I did not remember the couple saying that. I thought about how he was twice my age and my stepfather. How weird that anyone would think of us together as a couple. He often would say things that I found myself questioning later.

Tottenham is where most of my early memories with my baby brother were. We only saw my baby brother when we visited my mother and stepfather — time seemed to pass by way too fast between each visit. So, each time we saw my little brother, he had grown significantly. When my stepfather and mother came to pick us up from my father's house, my baby brother's face would light up with a big smile as soon as we entered the minivan. It was always such a heartwarming greeting and marked the beginning of our visit.

We thoroughly enjoyed camping with my mother, stepfather, and little brother. These trips were incredibly fun, and we explored many different places. My favourite trip was to Elora Gorge in Ontario. The rapids there were fantastic, and we went tubing down them. We particularly enjoyed a section of the rapids that was fast and turbulent, and we visited it repeatedly. On that trip, I fell off the tube and cracked a rib, but it was well worth the adventure.

During another one of our memorable family camping trips, my sisters and I helped teach my little brother how to walk. He skipped the crawling stage altogether, and we were incredibly proud of him. He was so eager to keep going that we held his hands and walked him all over the campground. His beaming smile showed how much he loved playing outside, especially in the parks.

My little brother was brilliant. He quickly learned the alphabet and seemed to have a photographic memory. He also loved watching cartoons. I remember us playing make-believe with him. His stuffed animals would magically "speak" in the voice of one of his sisters. He enjoyed these games and wanted to play them all the time. My little brother would yell from his bedroom at bedtime that he wanted a drink or a snack. He didn't want to go to sleep just yet.

As we returned to my father's house after our visits, my little brother's playful antics were a welcome distraction from the prevailing doom and gloom that seemed to fill the minivan each time.

This is a time in my life when I felt I bonded with my mother. She was a great mother to my little brother and us. She took care of all our needs. Sometimes, she would fall asleep in the front seat because the exhaustion set in from being a dedicated mother. She often smiled, and she appeared genuinely happy. I felt like I could have any conversation with her, which was the opposite of my relationship with my father. I also remember being a little jealous of my baby brother because he got to live with my mother full-time, and I could not.

SNOW

There comes a time when I am reborn,
As I descend from the sky towards the earth.
I know my time here is limited,
When and why, I do not know.

Under the bright, scorching sun,
I can feel myself fading oh so slowly,
Melting into the earth,
From which I initially fell.

My cool touch chills almost every living soul,
Yet young children seem to embrace me,
Play with me as much as they can.

I am stepped all over and pushed around,
Unwanted by some, cherished by others.
I know my presence is temporary,
Yet I always make sure to come at least once a year.

Written February 08, 1996

CHAPTER ELEVEN - NO FRIENDS OR FREEDOM

I WAS NOT ALLOWED TO have friends while growing up. Peers were not allowed to call the house—my father would say the house phone was only for emergencies. I could not go to my friends' homes, and they could not come to mine. I did not have freedom. It was not until I hit my preteens that my father finally allowed me to ride my bike to the corner store or around the block.

I attended Mary Ward Catholic School during my elementary years. The school had a strict regimen. I remember when the rule changed, the faculty could no longer hit the children with a ruler. I was in Grade 4. Up until that point, I had witnessed teachers hitting students. This also reinforced my belief that my home life was quite normal.

In third grade, I had snuck out. I was desperate to make friends. I bribed both my little sisters with my favourite stuffed dog. I told them they could have it if they did not tell our father that I had left. I slipped out our bedroom window. I walked and ran down Dorchester Road towards Fireman's Park. I remember being afraid the entire time. I repeatedly checked over my shoulder to ensure I did not see his vehicle. I made it to my friend's house. Her parents were surprised to see me. Either her parents called my father, or my sisters told him I had left because I remember him coming to their house to collect me. I was surprised he found me.

When I returned home, I knew that I would be punished. I remember repeating, "I must not sneak out of the house." My sisters also got in trouble. I blacked out a lot of what occurred, but I do remember feeling guilty that I had brought my sister into it and got them in trouble as well. This feeling was a recurring thought for me throughout my childhood years. I always felt I had to protect them because I was the oldest. I never snuck out of the house again.

I had few to no friends in elementary school. My peers bullied me all the time. I believed it was because of my appearance and maybe a little jealousy. My father often dropped us off at school on the trike he had built or in one of his many nice cars. He usually decked out his vehicles with ground-effect lighting, tinted windows, and decent stereo systems, which he always played loudly.

I had to wear glasses, and let me tell you, I couldn't stand them. I threw them away several times, like out of the van window at a gas station and into a school garbage can. Once, I chucked them into the school sandpit, a giant mud puddle in the middle of the schoolyard. My father was not happy with me. After school, he took me back with a rake and made me sift through that mud pit until I found them. My father always picked out my glasses for me; they were always these ugly things with thick lenses. I'm sure you've heard of the term "four eyes" before, right? I was teased constantly about them.

In sixth grade, I used to sneak into my grandmother's room and take her makeup and some of her clothes. I would then put them in my school bag and change in the bathroom once I arrived at school. Her clothes were usually too big for me as she was larger than I was. Looking back, I realize I probably looked silly, which might have given my classmates more reasons to make fun of me. I really wanted to express myself differently. I desperately wanted to fit in. My father wouldn't let me choose my outfits when we went shopping, and I wasn't allowed to wear makeup.

My father once cut my hair using an actual bowl, giving a "bowl cut" real meaning. He gave me all my haircuts, and I often looked ridiculous.

I was often excluded from school trips because my father would not allow me to go, and one that stands out is the Grade 8 "7-day camping trip." My class's excitement was notable as they prepared for the adventure. Despite my teacher's efforts to persuade my father to let me go, he did not allow me to. My teacher knew I wanted to go. During that week they were away, I felt isolated. When they returned, their stories painted vivid pictures of the fun and adventure they had, leaving me with intense feelings of resentment towards my father. His strict rules and controls hindered me from forming friendships, often leaving me sad and isolated.

Throughout my time at Mary Ward Elementary School, I endured relentless teasing from my peers. It was painful to realize that the verbal abuse I experienced at home was mirrored at school, where they were incredibly unkind. The kids often used me to climb their own social ladder, and I felt I was their stepping stone. If they hurt my feelings or made fun of me, it gained them some currency with the popular kids. All I ever wanted was to have friends and feel like I was a part of something. I often felt alone.

I attended A.N. Myer Secondary School for my 9th and 10th grades. My father did not allow me to date, but I was able to participate in one Grade 9 school dance. I was looking forward to it because some of my new friends I had made at high school were going. It gave me hope and a false reality that my high school years would be different. My father agreed to let me go if my stepmother accompanied me, and I agreed. At the dance, a boy asked me to slow dance with him. I accepted. My stepmother must have thought we were dancing too closely. Because when we got home, she told my father about it. From then on, I was not allowed to attend school dances. This incident crushed any hope that high school would be any different while living with my father.

While I was in high school, my father started his own roofing business. After school, I would walk over to his worksites to assist him. As his helper, I fetched the required supplies and tools and went up on the roofs. I learned how to rip off old roofs and put on new ones. My efforts seemed to please him. He remarked that my big chest (I had developed huge breasts during puberty) helped attract more business for him. He tasked me with approaching houses, knocking on doors, and distributing his business cards and pamphlets. I spent much quality time with my father during my grade nine and ten school years. This is the time where I have some good memories of us bonding.

My social life was different when I visited my mother's house in Tottenham. I was allowed freedom. Freedom to make and hang out with my friends. I met my first real best friend in Tottenham; we will call her Marianne. Marianne became my confidant. I talked to her about everything. We shared secrets and dreams. Marianne brought me up to speed on what being a teenager was really like. We spent most of our time at local parks and walking the streets of Tottenham. This is when I learned to talk to and flirt with boys. I had gained a little confidence. I met my first boyfriend. We held hands and shared that first awkward kiss.

On December 31, 1993, I had my first drinking experience. I was 15. We celebrated Marianne's upcoming birthday. My first drink was a mix of orange juice and vodka. We had a fantastic time bringing in the New Year in typical teenage style. We hung out with her older brother and his friend at her house. I liked her brother's friend. He was handsome. He gave me the nickname "DD." This was a reference to my large chest. I slept over at Marianne's house. I woke up the following day with my first hangover.

1994 was the year I was introduced to marijuana and hash for the first time. I attended bush parties with Marianne. I started experimenting with cigarettes. I got a taste of good old-fashioned freedom and immediately craved more. This was the year that significant changes would happen for me.

On May 25, 1994, I celebrated my sweet sixteenth. My mother made the day extra special for me. We had a party at Queen's Park in Niagara Falls. The couple of friends I had made at A.N. Myer and Marianne came. This was the first birthday party that my friends attended. I received many presents, but the one that stood out was a box of 16 roses, one of which was made of chocolate. It was my best birthday yet, making me realize the importance of friendships.

This experience and my time in Tottenham prompted me to consider leaving my father's house. Over the next few months, I carefully planned and prepared for this momentous decision to change my life—the decision to move out of my father's house and into my mother's.

FRIENDS

As summer bids adieu and autumn breezes sigh,
The leaves don hues of gold against the morning sky.
Like fleeting friends, they change with heedless grace,
As trust grows scarce, no one lends an ear in its place.

On the playground, the merry-go-round whirls, and twirls,
Spinning as fast as the tears of betrayal unfurl.
Friends come and go like passing trends,
While foes fill my thoughts and old friends attempt
to make amends.

In the winter wind, secrets softly swirl,
Whispering tales of new friendships and new souls are
starting to whirl.
Amidst the cold, I see a steady hand to hold,
New friendships spin madly, and stories remain untold.

Written on July 04, 2024

CHAPTER TWELVE – THE GREAT ESCAPE

THIS CHAPTER SIGNIFIES THE END of my childhood abuse and the beginning of my teenage and early adolescent years. My writing pattern will change as I have my journals to rely on to help me write about this next stage of my life. I am feeling relief and a deep sense of escape now that I have finished writing about my childhood abuse. I may touch on it going forward, but most of it has been released. It was difficult to relive and write about. This also marks the halfway point of my book. It's important to note that the next half of the book focuses on the aftermath and common issues that teenagers and young adults face when they come from significant childhood trauma.

It was the summer of 1994. My mother and stepfather had moved from Tottenham, Ontario, to Saint Catherines, Ontario. On the way home from a visit with my mother, I summoned up the courage to tell her that I did not want to go home and wanted to live with her instead. She advised me that I could make that decision because I was sixteen. My sisters became upset. They were apprehensive and concerned about my father's actions when they entered the house without me. They were not ready and did not want to leave him. I felt guilty that I would not be there to protect them. My heart was pounding, and my fear was in my throat. We pulled up to the front of my father's house, and I crouched low to hide. Both my sisters got out. I did not leave the minivan. I remember being afraid that he might come out and chase us as we drove away. I was finally leaving him. I was escaping.

I spent the days and nights after my great escape looking over my shoulder. I would not go to his house to pick up or drop off my sisters. I remember being scared most of the time. My sisters shared with me that my father had thrown his crack pipe down on the living room table and told them that this was where everything was going. He stated that he did not care anymore. He placed the blame on me. He told them he felt he had nothing else to live for because I had left.

This is when I found out that my father had a real drug habit. As a side note, years prior, he had been in a terrible car accident. A woman had rear-ended him. His story is that she was trying to commit suicide by driving into the back of him. He often complained about back pain. I remember him asking us to walk on his back while he lay down on the floor. He used pain medication. This could have been the start of him using street drugs. Often, people become addicted to street drugs after prolonged use of pain medication. I remember that he was highly paranoid of being caught working odd jobs. He would always be on the lookout. I believe he received a decent settlement from this accident, which is how he started the roofing business.

My sisters told me that my father drove to my mother's house and sat with them across the street, watching and waiting. They said that he had brought one of his shotguns. He was either going to attempt to kidnap me or shoot us. My father had utterly lost his mind. The first month after leaving my father, I would hide in my mother's duplex's basement and peek out the blinds. I was terrified. When I would go outside of my mother's house, I would be watchful for my father. I was afraid that he would show up. Sometimes, I felt I had seen him; I would make a full-out dash back to my mother's house.

I did have to have one phone conversation with my father, stepmother, and paternal family. I remember my father crying and begging for me to come home. I stood up to him for the first time in my life. I told him I did not want to and shared my reasons with him. I told him that he had been abusive and controlling. I mentioned that he did not let me have friends or date boys. My father used his famous line. "Do you girls only remember the bad times? Why don't you girls remember the good times?" This was his way of not talking about it and changing the subject. He brought up the times he took us boating, to the park to fly kites, and out for ice cream. Like these times had made up for the abuses we endured. He did not like that he could not manipulate me into coming back. He told me that I was killing him. He handed the phone off to my stepmother.

My stepmother told me that my father was not doing well. She stated that he might harm himself. I told her that she knew what had happened in that house, and I had made up my mind. I would not be coming back. My stepmother called me a witch in Italian. She told me I was being selfish. I did not care what my evil stepmother thought. We were not fond of my stepmother. She did not take care of us well. What I remember about her was when she would make us plain bread and cheese sandwiches for school lunches. She broke things but did not take ownership. She would blame us, and then we would be punished for it. She did not want my father to hit her, but she did not mind if we were hit. She was one of the adults who did nothing when we were abused. It is my opinion that she was selfish.

I did speak to my grandmother and aunt, but I cannot remember what they said. When I left my father's house, I knew I had to cut ties with my paternal family. He would ensure they did not speak to me. They seemed to always listen to him. Neither my grandmother nor my aunts or uncles crossed him. That family stuck together and kept each other's secrets. In my experience, they had never stepped in and stopped my father.

About a month after my great escape, my sisters also decided to move in with my mother. They refused to go back to our father's house. We went to the Saint Catherine's Police Station, filed a report, and tried to obtain a restraining order. We informed the authorities about my father's actions, including coming to my mother's house with a gun, and expressed our fear of what he might do. For the first time, we spoke about the abuse we had endured. We felt anxious, nervous, and guilty about revealing the secrets.

My middle sister told the police that my father had burned her. My younger sister and I also told the truth and supported her statement. The police informed us that they knew he was dangerous but couldn't take any action unless he did something illegal. They also said that my middle sister couldn't press charges for being thrown into hot water because of a legal term called double jeopardy. Once someone has been acquitted and found not guilty, they could not be charged with the same offence again. The police must have charged him when my mother took him to court. They explained that my middle sister and I could legally choose to live with our mother, but if my father wanted to take my younger sister back, he could. We left the police station feeling disappointed and discouraged. We found the experience left us feeling uncomfortable.

I think the police did talk with my father, warning him to stay away. I did not see him again for about a year. My sisters said they had seen him around the neighbourhood and near their new school. During that year, there was a break-in at my mother's house. They called the police to check the house because it was apparent that someone had been there. My sisters explained to the police that there had been multiple sightings of my father around the neighbourhood. There was a fear that he might attempt to grab my youngest sister, as she was not of age to decide where she wanted to live.

I have reason to believe that I broke into the house while they were not home. As you will find out in the next chapter, I moved out. I think I stole alcohol and cigarettes. I am not positive about this memory, but there is an inkling that it is a possibility.

ANGEL'S FLIGHT

As I tread the path to my slumber's embrace,
I envision my angels taking flight with grace.
In my mind's eye, their celestial forms unfurl,
As they carry me on a wondrous flying whirl.

High above, we glide through the tranquil night,
Stars shimmering like jewels, casting their gentle light.
The cool night air caresses my skin so tender,
As we soar, the wind whispers a serene surrender.

In this vivid mental flight, calmness surrounds me,
Like a voyager on a boundless, peaceful sea.
With angelic guides, solace unfurls its comforting wings,
Lulling me into a state where tranquillity sings.

Written on July 05, 2024

CHAPTER 13 - LOSING MY VIRTUE

IN SEPTEMBER 1994, I TRANSFERRED from A. N. Myer to West Park Secondary School. I was in Grade 11 and was no longer in Niagara Falls. However, I did not spend much time at this new school. I made up excuses to my teachers and principals about why I could not attend, and I even lied to the school counsellor about being physically abused at home to keep her from calling my mother and stepfather. I went through a phase of lying during this new period of my life. I had a newfound freedom, and I embraced it. I transformed from being a saint into a hellion. I skipped school, made a lot of new friends, experimented with drugs and alcohol, and dated boys. I lost my virginity. I had been so sheltered my entire life up until this point. I completely lost my bearings, and in the process, I also lost my virtues.

When I skipped school, I often hung out with friends and smoked marijuana daily. We would hang out at a few townhomes in the complex next to the school. A few of my friends lived there. I was often too stoned to attend. I remember being in class this one time. It was History 11. The teacher called me out in front of the whole class. He asked me if everything was looking hazy through my eyes. I knew exactly what he meant. I did not attend his class very much after he made that comment.

In February of 1995, my mother and stepfather discovered that I had more absences than days attended at school. They sat me down and gave me an ultimatum. My stepfather did most of the talking, as he tended to do. He went on about the "ladder of life," falling down a few rungs and then having to climb back up. Blah, blah, blah. Essentially, I took away from the conversation that I needed to spend less time with my friends. My stepfather even went as far as to say they would escort me to each class to ensure I attended. When I questioned the new rules and what would happen if I disagreed, they told me I could leave if I didn't like it. I distinctly remember thinking that nobody was going to take away my freedom ever again.

I went straight to my bedroom, packed my clothing and belongings into three full garbage bags, and left. I was so adamant about leaving that I dragged those garbage bags for blocks to my girlfriend's house. I had to carry two bags down a few yards and then go back, grab the other one, and drag it to where I left the original two. I remember this being an arduous and lengthy process. I finally arrived at my girlfriend's house. She lived in the complex near the school. I knew that she would let me live there. I already had spent so much time there. I ended up quitting school shortly after. Partying and hanging out with friends were far more essential. I believe I was making up for lost time.

I lived at my girlfriend's house for a few months. Her mother had Schizophrenia, so the home was unsupervised. A bunch of us teenagers lived there. One of them was my boyfriend. We will call him Brian. We partied daily. It was loud and obnoxious. A lot of alcohol consumption and marijuana smoking went on. The basement was set up with a black light, and we often played loud music, such as "Sepultura, Nirvana, Pearl Jam, and the Ramones."

There had been numerous complaints from neighbours. The police arrived at the townhouse and told my friends they could no longer stay there. My friends were escorted out and warned by the officers that they were not allowed back in the town-house. At the time, I wasn't there. When I arrived at the house and knocked, one of my friends opened the door. She had been hiding in one of the upstairs bedroom closets and explained what had happened. I quickly packed some of my clothes and belong-ings into a laundry hamper, leaving behind many other items. We had no choice but to go as we were not supposed to be there.

As my two friends and I were leaving the townhouse, we were arrested. I was charged with "unlawful entry of a dwelling home." The police handcuffed me, put me in a police car, and took me to the police station. I was terrified, as I had never been charged with anything before. During the questioning, I overheard them saying they would make the experience difficult for me because I was the daughter of the infamous (insert father's name).

While sitting in the cell, I remembered my father and I sitting in his van at Fireman's Park (when I lived with him) a few summers earlier. He was asleep in the bed in the back while I sat in the driver's seat, organizing new school supplies for myself and my sisters. It was just my father and me. It was the summer before I started high school. A police officer pulled in behind the van. I saw the officer get out of the cruiser, walk up along the side of the van, and knock on the passenger window. He advised me to wake my father. My father explained to the officer that he was taking a nap. My father was asked for his licence. The police officer went back to his vehicle. My father had a police scanner (He always listened to the police scanner). He told me to turn it on quickly. I did. We listened while the officer called it in. They advised the police officer that my father was dangerous, might be armed, and to approach with caution. I turned it off when I saw the officer leaving the cruiser to return to the van. He came back and told my father to leave the area at once.

While I was in cells, the police advised my mother and step-father that I was arrested, or I might have called my mother and told her. They came to the police station to see me. I was ushered into a small holding cell. I could see my mother and stepfather through a glass window. I remember putting my hand up and my mother putting hers up to meet mine. I was upset and crying. I felt a massive injustice about why I had been arrested. The officers told me that they would release me into the custody of my mother and stepfather. I refused to go with them, as I felt uncomfortable around my stepfather.

I was transferred from Saint Catherines to Hamilton, Ontario, and spent the night at a Hamilton jail. At the time, the prison was transferring all the female prisoners from the facility to an all-female facility. I was the only female. I remember men banging on the pipes, communicating with each other that a new female had arrived. This was scary, and I was overwhelmed. My cell contained a bed with a thin mattress. There was a toilet and sink in the corner of the small cell.

The following morning, a guard escorted me to a communal area. The room was full of grown men. There were long tables and chairs. It appeared like a giant cafeteria. A few young men approached me. They introduced themselves and advised me to stick with them. They would keep me safe and protect me. They pointed out inmates that I should not look at or talk to. After breakfast, I returned to my cell. Soon afterwards, a guard came and got me. He loaded me in a transport van.

I would not spend another night there. I was transported back to the Courthouse in Saint Catherine's, Ontario. That afternoon, I went in front of a judge. I was remanded into the custody of my mother and stepfather. I had a set of conditions. One was that I had to reside in their home as I was 16 years old.

TICKING SOUND

Inside my mind, a ticking sound I hear,
Time seems to pass me by as my fears draw near,
My thoughts are echoed like a distant clock.
To the beat of my own inner tick-tock.

This ticking sound I hear doesn't seem to go away,
I find my body following along with a rhythmic sway.
My mind hones into this inner ticking sound,
As I search for a choice that I think is meant to be found.

Is the sound, the soft reminder of my time that is left,
Will I be able to face the challenge or be left feeling bereft?
Will the choice I make hold steady and true,
Or will I falter when the time runs out and not know what to do?

Written on July 06, 2024

CHAPTER FOURTEEN - STEPFATHER

I BELIEVE THIS IS THE time I need to explain what happened with my stepfather that made me so uncomfortable that I was willing to spend the night in jail instead of with him. My stepfather was my second abuser. As an adult, I have chosen not to have a relationship with him. The first time he abused me, I was young. I was 9 or 10 years old. This was in the early days when my mother and stepfather travelled from Ottawa to Niagara Falls to visit us. We were spending the night at one of my maternal Aunt's houses. I had taken NeoCitran because I was ill. The NeoCitran did not sit well with me. To this day, I will not drink it. It was the first time that I vomited through my nose. It burned something awful. I was awake in the middle of the night because I could not sleep due to being sick. My stepfather came to keep me company.

My sisters and I were sleeping in one of the bedrooms. My stepfather took me there and told me he could help me fall back asleep. He lay down next to me, and he put my hand on his hairy chest. He had coarse, curly, dark hair. He told me I would fall asleep easier if I rubbed his chest. Even as I am writing this, I am feeling disgusted and repulsed. This man made me feel so gross. I despised him. He knew where I came from and what I endured, but I believe he could not help himself.

I had several conversations with my mother about my stepfather through my teenage years. I told her often that he made me uncomfortable. His touch and hugs would give me the heebie-jeebies. She had multiple conversations with him. He told her I was imagining it. He stated that this is how he showed me that he loved me and that I was not used to it because of my father. This is the messaging I received repeatedly. Time would reveal that I was not imagining it. I believe to this day that he was attempting to groom me for other things.

My stepfather groomed his victims. He liked young girls. There were many victims that I knew about, including my middle sister. When I left my father at sixteen and moved into my mother's house. My stepfather and mother were on a break. He was not living with her. This helped me make my decision to move in with her. It was one of the significant reasons. My friend, Marianne (from Tottenham), had accused my stepfather of attempting to sleep with her. This happened just before my Great Escape.

I had not heard from Marianne, so I phoned her. She told me what had occurred. It happened during one of my last visits to my mother's house. Marianne had come out to Saint Catherines to sleep over. I had gone home to my father's house, and it was decided that Marianne would spend one more night before being dropped off at her home in Tottenham. My stepfather went downstairs. He approached Marianne. He groped her, touched her inappropriately and asked her to sleep with him. Marianne refused him. Marianne told me it was a horrible experience that left her afraid and violated. She told me she wanted to press charges but was not going to because she did not want to hurt me or my mother. This incident changed Marianne and my friendship. I have and will always blame my stepfather for that.

My stepfather told my mother that Marianne, who was 15, had been flirting with him. He told her that he could not help himself. Marianne's natural personality was charming, friendly, outgoing, and energetic. She did not find my stepfather remotely attractive. She looked at him like a safe adult, her friend's stepfather. There was no world where Marianne would have flirted with my stepfather.

My stepfather told my mother that it was a mistake. He felt like he did it because he was going through a midlife crisis. My stepfather had theories about older men being attracted to younger women. He shared them with me all the time. Something about how a woman changed after having a baby, which made her less attractive. I did not pay much attention to him when he talked because it was often long-winded and did not make sense. He thought of himself as a brilliant man. I still believe to this day that he shared these uncomfortable conversations with me because he, again, was attempting to groom me.

My mother and stepfather were separated for a few months. But when my sisters moved in, my stepfather also moved back in. My mother eventually forgave him, and they got back together. I was not happy when this happened. I remember feeling disappointed and upset. I felt that Marianne and my experiences were ignored. I believe this reinforced the fact that I was indeed alone and that my mother was not going to protect me.

So, after my arrest, I was not thrilled after the judge decided I would reside with my mother and stepfather. I felt extremely uncomfortable. After a few weeks of being there, I was in the kitchen when my stepfather came in and hugged me. He instantly gave me the no feeling. He leaned in and kissed me. He stuck his tongue in my mouth. I was repulsed and immediately had to leave. I called one of my male friends who knew my history with my stepfather. He came and picked me up. When I spoke to my mother about him doing this, the message I received was that I imagined it because of the incident between my stepfather and my friend, Marianne. My stepfather denied it, and I was told I had made it up. I know what a tongue feels like when it is invading your mouth. I know that I felt like vomiting after the incident.

I decided not to return to my mother's house, breaking my court condition. I would not live with my stepfather. My mother did not tell the authorities that I had left. I lived at my male friend's house for a few weeks before we all decided to rent an apartment together: my friend, his girlfriend, my boyfriend (Brian), and I.

I still had to go to court for my charge. My mother would come with me. The charge was finally dropped as it was found I had been charged falsely. I remember this day after court well. My mother and I drove to a secluded location. She told me that my stepfather, she, and both my sisters were moving to Vancouver, BC. She explained that this was partly because of the fear surrounding my father. She told me I could come with them if I wanted to.

I bawled my eyes out. I told her I could not go. I could not live with my stepfather. I explained to her that he had made me uncomfortable too many times. I was afraid that he might do something more. I had to protect myself. I told her not to go and to leave him. We both cried in that car together. We held each other's hands. When she dropped me off at my house, I thought she had listened and understood. I thought she was going to leave him.

In the late spring of 1995, they all moved to BC together (including my stepfather), leaving me in Saint Catherines, Ontario, to fend for myself and learn how to live without my sisters. I had just turned 17. I do not believe that my mother asked anyone if she could legally take my sisters out of the province. She just did it.

FLASHBACK

A cool, breezy evening, having a peaceful time; slowly, memories came creeping into my mind.

The images slowly emerged, coming into view. A man full of rage and frustration grew.

My memories rapidly changed into reality. Leaving behind my realm of actuality.

I could feel him brutally hurting me so. I can only scream and cry out loud to let you know.

As this man betrays my rights and steals my control, I doubt that when he is done, I will feel whole.

In the far distance, I hear a gentle voice. Calling me back to the place where I still have a choice.

Repeatedly, I beg the man to stop hurting me so. Waiting for him to finish because I know he will go.

He finally leaves me alone in the dark. I lay curled up, and my surroundings feel quite stark.

My eyes are shut tightly, and I feel I am unable to wake; I feel the bruises deep inside of me, and I feel my body start to shake.

When my eyes open, my visions become too clear. I see the owner of that gentle voice, his face full of fear.

My breathing is rapid and short, my heart pounding so fast. I wait while I feel the chills, sweat, and feelings might last.

I sit bundled up and dare not to move out of his embrace. I know it is over, and I do not want to relive that trauma in that horrible space.

Written January 20, 1996

CHAPTER FIFTEEN – THE STRUGGLE WAS REAL

IN JUNE OF 1995, BRIAN and I decided to relocate to British Columbia following my family's departure. The absence of my mother, brother, and sisters was deeply felt. Our journey took us from Ontario to BC via bus; as it turned out, one of our friends decided to make the move simultaneously. The trek through the middle provinces was rather uneventful, with vast stretches of flat land and an endless sky. However, the scenery underwent a remarkable transformation once we reached the border of Alberta and BC. The sight of mountains for the first time left me in awe, and the blending colours of the valleys, trees, and mountains created a true spectacle.

We spent a couple of weeks in BC with my family when we arrived. Brian and I felt uncomfortable and became homesick. We decided we did not like it and returned to Saint Catherines, Ontario. My stepfather paid for our flights back home.

I remember arriving at the Toronto Pearson International Airport. Brian and I had no money. We attempted to walk from Toronto back to Saint Catherines. We tried to hitchhike along the way, but no one would stop and pick us up. We walked along-side Highway 401 and 407 (Ontario's busiest highways) for a long time, dragging our luggage behind us. We made it to Rebecca Street Bus Terminal. I want to give you an idea of the distance. It was approximately sixty-five kilometres (thirty-nine miles) away. It would typically take you forty-two minutes to drive. It took us most of the day to walk. Our feet were sore, and we were tired. Eventually, my maternal uncle paid for our bus tickets. We were able to get a bus from Hamilton to Saint Catherines.

Back in Saint Catherines, we bounced around to various places until settling into an apartment in the early summer of 1995. This was the first place I had lived since moving out of my mother's house that I could call my own. We furnished it. I remember finding an old light oak stereo cabinet that played records. It was my favourite piece of furniture. I worked odd jobs at farm fields to earn extra money. I was also on welfare. The welfare agency knew that I did not have parents that I could ask for help at the time. I was not speaking to my father because I was afraid of him. My mother was on the other side of the country. Welfare was not generally given to teenagers, but they gave it to me.

I found an organization (house) in Saint Catherines that helped street youth. The organization was called The RAFT (Resource Association for Teens). I visited there regularly. Brian and I did not have much money. We were poor. I also was struggling mentally as I did not know how to deal with the emotions, triggers, or trauma. I had "freakout sessions." Also known as "flashbacks." I looked to the counsellors at The RAFT for help. I spent hours in their offices. We received groceries from them, and I browsed the clothing donations to find clothing I liked. They had washing machines. I often did my laundry there. The RAFT was a resource and a haven that I used regularly. I phoned them once as a young adult woman and thanked them for their services. They really supported me through an extremely challenging time when I often found myself struggling to survive.

Another organization that I used was the Ozanam Center. They served food to people experiencing poverty. I went there for coffee and meals. I met a man there who shared a heartbreaking story with me about how he became homeless. There had been a fire in which he lost his wife and two girls. He was depressed and did not know how to go on living. He lived on the streets of Saint Catherines. We became acquaintances. I found his story eye-opening. I realized then that individuals sometimes have probable reasons to live the way they do. At times, I find myself thinking if I could sit and listen to some of these individuals' life stories – would I find that they have come from abuse and trauma? Did they also feel lost and unable to find their way out?

There was also a mentally ill man who went to the Ozanam Center. I ran into him a few times. He thought I was his ex-wife. He immediately became angry when he saw me, and he charged at me. The staff saved my life a few times. One time, he threw his coffee mug at me, screaming at me and threatening to kill me. After that incident, I often walked the other way. I wanted to avoid him at all costs.

I struggled with buying cigarettes as I was poor and did not have money. I remember collecting cigarette butts off the street. I bummed cigarettes off anyone who would give me one, and I often found myself standing outside the supermarket asking strangers for a cigarette. One day, my friend and I were standing outside a No-Frills store when a woman with a dog approached us. She asked if we could watch her dog while she went into the store to buy groceries. We agreed, with the understanding that she would give us some cigarettes afterwards. When she returned, she invited us back to her house. She said that she wanted to have a drink with us. She also said that she would give us some free marijuana. Unfortunately, we accepted her invitation and went with her.

At her house, she invited my friend and me into her bathroom. She asked us to pull down our pants to inspect the shaving jobs we had done on our privates. She told us about an opportunity to make money in Niagara Falls on Clifton Hill. She said it was a professional gig. A private escort business. The way she explained what the job entailed – she made it sound very lucrative and sexy. She introduced us to her boyfriend. They gave us a free bag of marijuana and a few packs of cigarettes with the promise that we would return. My friend and I ran out of there so fast with the thought that we would never go back. In retrospect, I escaped a terrifying situation.

The relationship between Brian and me was ending. He was cheating on me with multiple women. I remember catching him in the act at the apartment. He was sleeping with my friend, who rented another apartment in the same building. She lived on the same floor. I had gone looking for Brian. I could hear them having sex while I stood outside the door. I peered through the peephole. I knocked on the door and interrupted them. I confronted them about it. Brian and I broke up. He immediately moved out.

After he moved out, I ran into her in the hallway. I was entering my apartment, and she was coming out of hers. We started arguing from opposite ends of the hallway. She called me a whore. I found this quite insulting and ironic as she had been caught sleeping with my boyfriend. She was a large teenage girl, heavier set and more robust than I was. We were yelling at each other. She came barreling at me. I fought back. My head bounced off the walls and floor a few times. I lost my mind, and the incident blurred. I remember the ambulance arriving. She had called them because she was worried. The fight had ended, but I was having one of my "freakout sessions." I was taken to the hospital.

After I was released, I moved out of that apartment immediately. I did not feel safe there anymore. I left all the furniture behind, including that oak stereo cabinet.

I moved into another friend's house in mid-July 1995. Her parents rented me a bedroom. At this point, I was now a single teenager. Many boys showed interest in me. Because I was partying so much, I put myself in some very sticky situations. I was raped twice by two different men during this time.

The first was a supposed friend who forced himself on me. We were at the house that he lived in. I hung out at this house often. A bunch of boys lived there. He was one of those boys interested in me, but I was not attracted to him. I told him I was not interested, but he did not listen. He ignored my continuous attempts to stop him from going further. He continued to take off my clothing, and I let it happen because I knew I could not fight him off. I went to the blank space in my mind and waited for it to end. I believe the blank space was an imaginary place I had invented as a little girl.

The second was a grown man. He was built like a brick house and was thirty-eight years old. A close friend and I were partying with her boyfriend and friends down by a gorge. I remember sitting in the back seat of a vehicle with him. He put his hand on my thigh and moved it upward toward my private area. I told him to stop. He did. I remember feeling uncomfortable around him.

Somehow, we ended up back at one of the men's apartments. I was in a bedroom. This man was on top of me. I begged for him to stop. My close friend was in the next room, and she ignored my cries and screams. I attempted to push him off, but he was much stronger than me. I remember giving up and laying there staring up at the ceiling while being violated. I remember thinking, let him do it, it will end, and you can leave. I never forgave my friend for not helping me.

I blamed myself, too, for putting myself in these situations. I should have known better. I think sexual assault victims often blame themselves. But the blame truly lies with the abusers. I think that I had low self-esteem, and the abusers took advantage of situations where I was not in complete control, or they felt they could overpower me. These rapes left me violated and scared. They happened back-to-back within months of each other.

It was August 1995, and I felt my life was falling apart in Saint Catherines. I had been raped twice, I felt alone, and girls who hung out with my ex-boyfriend, Brian, wanted to fight me. The girls did not like that I talked to others about how he had cheated and how things had ended. Things felt like they were spiralling out of control. I was at an event. A mini rave that someone put together in an old building when these girls showed up with my ex-Brian. There was a woman a little older than me. She had a reputation for being a fighter. She was trained in Martial Arts. The group had circled me outside the event. She was standing at the head of the group. She called me out.

My initial reaction was to run, but I did not. I knew that if I did, they would never stop harassing me. I fought her. I remember kicking and punching her. She grabbed my hair. I grabbed her hair back. We stayed locked together for a few minutes. Finally, we both let go of each other's hair. The fight was over. Neither of us won. I went back to the place where I was staying. I did not feel safe anymore. I realized I had to leave Saint Catherines.

THIS OR THAT

From one place to the next,
From this to that,
From father to mother,
Is it always just tit for tat?

In love's embrace once more,
I've moved to be with him,
Will I stay steady and sure,
Or sink back into shadows grim?

He appears almost too perfect,
But what if it's all just a show?
Am I ready to take that step,
When I'm unsure who's friend or foe?

My life is precious, don't be mistaken,
I leaped without looking around,
His feelings seem deep and unshaken,
May this be the love I've finally found.

From there to here,
From fiction to truths exact,
From a smile to a tear,
Is it always so exact?

Written January 27, 1998

CHAPTER SIXTEEN – CRACK AND COCAINE

IN AUGUST 1995, I WENT to the Welfare Office in Saint Catherines. While at the counter, I looked over and saw him. My father was standing in line at the front desk. I was super nervous. At first, I wanted to run and hide. But then, looking at him, I felt sorry for him. He looked unhealthy – skinny and dishevelled. He looked over at me but did not appear to recognize me. It was like he was staring straight through me. I questioned myself why I had thought that I should approach him. Why should I even speak to him? I came to the quick conclusion that he did not look like the scary monster I had left. He appeared sad and vulnerable. I felt sorry for him. Secretly, I had longed to have a good relationship with my father.

I walked up to him and said, "Hi, Dad." He did not register that it was me. I could not believe it. It had been one year since I had left him. I told him it was me, his eldest daughter. He appeared shocked. My father was deep in his cocaine/crack habit. We proceeded to talk for a bit. He had fallen on tough times. He no longer had his roofing business. He had spent all the money he had received from the settlement. He offered to drive me home. I accepted. When he dropped me off, we agreed on another meeting.

After this run-in, I started visiting with him regularly. The visits began with short coffee dates and small talk. Soon, I was going for long drives with him and long walks at Crystal Beach and Port Colbourne. Over time, he did not appear scary anymore. I do not know how it happened, but I soon agreed to move back into the Dorchester house in Niagara Falls. I felt I was in desperate need of a change. I also felt I needed some normality or what I considered normal as I had grown up with this man. Looking back, I do not think a healthy, well-rounded person would have made my choice.

In September 1995, I returned to my childhood home on Dorchester Road. The house was the same as I remembered it. I soon discovered that my father had been living alone with my stepmother. My grandmother had moved out and was in the process of selling the house. My father refused to leave. He was squatting in my grandmother's home. The rest of the family was not speaking to him. He was using drugs daily. I wondered what living with him must have been like for the family while I was gone.

The upstairs was empty and bare—all the furniture had been moved out. The only rooms that remained furnished were my father's area in the basement. We set up a bedroom for me in another section of the basement. I would watch him and my stepmother using their drugs daily. My stepmother would pick at fluff in the carpet on her hands and knees, and my father would spend his time in the upstairs bathroom, sitting in a tub, picking away at his arms. He thought bugs were crawling and living in his skin. The crack did not help his paranoia.

Soon, I would join them. My curiosity got the better of me. At first, my father would give me his crack rocks to hold on to. He did not trust my stepmother. I kept them safe for him. He knew I would not do it. My father would eventually teach me how to do it. We would then do it together. I found myself liking the high at first. We would go for long drives and sit together in his car, hiding in a parking lot. We reminisced about his childhood and mine. He would, at times, admit some of his wrongdoings. He also shared with me about his father. I felt we were bonding. I have to repeat what I just wrote; my father and I were bonding while doing crack/cocaine together. This was so unhealthy, but I did not see it that way then.

This time with him gave me a different view of him as a man. He was stripped down to his raw insecurities. He did not appear powerful anymore. I was not afraid of him. What I saw was a drug addict. He seemed weak and broken. He was very skinny. His face was gaunt. He would beg others for money to feed his habit. We once went to my uncle's apartment. My uncle had Schizophrenia. My father repeatedly phoned him while waiting outside his apartment, begging him for money. My uncle eventually caved and gave it to him.

I stopped using the drug shortly afterwards. I did not like the feeling it gave me. I was lucky in this aspect because I could have become heavily addicted myself. I found that I am the type of person who, if I do not like something, can easily quit it. I have found that I do not like being under the influence of drugs that take away my self-control or my thoughts. This has been my saving grace with many drugs throughout my teenage and early adolescent years. I attempted to help my father stop using crack. If anyone has a loved one who is addicted to hard drugs, they will know that it is impossible. The person needs to want to stop on their own.

Eventually, I convinced him to leave my grandmother's house and move into an apartment together. My grandmother finally was able to sell the Dorchester house. I helped him start mending his relationships with other family members. I encouraged him to reach out and start talking to them. We would visit my grandmother at her new home. She was living at my paternal great-grandmother's house, which had passed away. My grandmother had inherited it.

Visiting that house brought back old memories for me of my great-grandmother. She was a short older lady with white hair. She had a big chest (which is where I think I had inherited mine). She only spoke Italian. When we visited her as kids, she would constantly bring out food. She always had homemade Italian food and desserts. She constantly kept you fed. She would say, "Mangia, Mangia," which meant "Eat, Eat." Or she would say, "Buona, Buona." In my childhood, I thought this meant "Dip, Dip," but I recently learned that it meant "Enjoy, Enjoy."

I had slept over at her house a few times when I was little. She would give me warm milk just before bed. I remember sneaking a phone call to my mother at one of my great-grandmother's sleepovers. She told my father and grandmother about it. I got in trouble. I also remember that I broke her window blind (or took responsibility for breaking it). I was punished by my father for that as well. My great-grandmother had natural hardwood in her living room and dining room. Us girls would help her wax it. I remember it being a big job.

Enough about memories. I was helping my father mend his family relationships. My grandmother hosted the family get-togethers. My uncles, aunts, and cousins were back in my life. The visits there were awkward. It often felt like there was an elephant in the room – my father's current drug habit, the secrets of the abuse, and the choice I had made to abandon the family. My relationship with them never returned to how it was before I ran away. I felt that my father and I were being judged constantly. There was always an odd feeling at those family get-togethers.

I attempted to share and have conversations with my grand-mother on numerous occasions about why I had left. She would reach out to help me with rides and grocery shopping. I hoped she would honestly and openly discuss the past abuses in that house on Dorchester Road. But she could or would not. She would often state that our conversations gave her anxiety after-wards. She said on numerous occasions that she could not speak about it because it would cause her to feel like she was going to have a heart attack.

I remember sharing with my grandmother that my father had introduced me to crack/cocaine. She seemed upset by it but made excuses for him. I found my relationship with her strained.

My father and I found a quaint two-bedroom apartment to move into. My stepmother came along with us. The apartment had character, especially my bedroom. My room had an arched roof. It was an attic/loft type of room. I loved it. I set it up with my things. It felt like home. I lived with them for a few months. My father did not abuse me during this time.

COURAGE

Gather all your strength!
Make it through each day.
Go to great length!
To change it to your way.

Hold your head up high!
Be proud of who you are.
Figure out what is in the lie!
And distance yourself from afar.

Don't teach yourself not to love!
Just learn from your past.
Make sure you push and shove!
To get yourself to the top fast.

You can make it in this world!
It is what you make it to be.
Just detour past the hurt hurled
And your future, you will see.

Written September 28, 2003

CHAPTER SEVENTEEN – UNFORBIDDEN LOVE

I MET A MAN IN October 1995. For privacy reasons, let's call him Grayson. Grayson was five years older than me and was roommates with the boyfriend of one of my friends. Initially, I didn't like Grayson as I found him chauvinistic and a bit controlling. I didn't find him attractive, and during one of our early interactions, I felt he was forceful sexually. I felt taken advantage of, and he did not listen to my objections. Looking back, I should have trusted my initial gut instinct, but unfortunately, I did not.

In the following month, Grayson was persistent. I ignored his phone calls and didn't visit him. He surprised me by showing up at the employment program I was attending. He brought gifts. He even made me a homemade cassette tape of love songs and wrote me love letters. Eventually, he won me over, and on November 23, 1995, Grayson became my boyfriend.

Shortly after we started dating, I packed my belongings and moved out of my father's house and in with Grayson. My father did not like him. A Romeo and Juliet type of love story pushed me towards him more. There was a history between his uncle and my paternal uncle. They had beef over an old flame. Our uncles had physically fought at a bar when they were young men. The families did not like each other. It felt like it was forbidden.

Grayson was a smooth talker. He was the type of guy who paid close attention to what you said. His strong quality was his communication ability. He made you comfortable, and I felt I could share anything with him. He made you feel like he understood you. He had past trauma with his family. He could be very endearing and kind when he wanted to. He often made me feel protected against others, but soon, I would find out I needed protection from him.

Approximately one month after dating, Grayson disappeared to Saint Catherines for three days. Our roommate and I could not reach him, and Grayson did not contact me. I spent those three days in tears and worried sick about what had happened to him. When Grayson came back, I was relieved that he was safe. It was the first of the month, and we owed our portion of the rent. Grayson said he did not have it. He had spent all the rent money.

I found out that Grayson had been with another woman and had been on a drinking bender during his three-day disappearance. As a result, Grayson got kicked out because his roommate was fed up with Grayson's behaviour - not having the rent money and constant lies. This strained my relationship with my friend and her boyfriend (the roommate). They warned me not to move in with Grayson, but I did. I was willing to give him another chance. For some reason, I believed he could change if I tried harder. Later, I discovered that Grayson had stolen more money from our roommate, including one of the roommate's blank cheques.

Grayson and I found a small upper-level apartment to rent. On May 25, 1996, I went out for my birthday. Grayson had allowed me to go with my girlfriend on my own. Yes, I am aware that I said it was allowed. We went dancing at a local bar. I loved dancing. I had only turned 18 but was able to sneak into the bar. When I arrived home, Grayson immediately became aggressive with me. He accused me of cheating on him. He threw me around our bedroom and hit me several times. He choked me. He forced himself on me and raped me. To him, I was his property and the one with whom he could do whatever he wanted.

A neighbour who lived downstairs came up and banged on our door. He yelled at Grayson to stop abusing me. Grayson immediately went downstairs with a bat and banged on his door. I remember chasing after him, telling him to stop. The neighbour did not open the door. Grayson yelled at the neighbour through the door to mind his own business. This neighbour came up later with a bottle of alcohol as a peace offering. The neighbour apologized to Grayson, and they drank together.

After my birthday incident, we moved into a motel and were given the job of running it for the owner. It was a sweet gig, and we were making decent money. We employed my stepmother to clean the rooms. My father visited me at the motel regularly. During one of his visits, he told me that a female that he had dated had been murdered. This was my father's ex-girlfriend, whom he supposedly threw in hot water. My father told me that the police found her body in Welland, Ontario. He also shared that she was pregnant at the time. She had been visiting his friend (a dealer) around the time that she went missing. He also commented offhand about what a vehicle would look like with a body in a trunk. I found the conversation concerning that I phoned the police and told an officer about it. He stated he would investigate it. I obviously thought that my father was capable of committing murder. Nothing ever came of this, and my father was never charged.

In July 1996, Grayson and I discussed that I visit my mother, sister, and brother in BC. Grayson permitted me to go and paid for my return airline ticket. During the one-week visit to BC, I found I enjoyed myself. My family appeared to have settled into their new life. I spent quality time with my sisters. I hung out with some of my sister's friends. I felt like I could act more my age. With Grayson, I felt older for some reason. I had an odd sense of freedom, but I could not put my finger on it. This was the first time I met my future husband, Colin. (At the time, I did not think I would marry him. He was not even on my radar). I did not get to know Colin well, as I was only there for a week. My sisters knew him through a mutual friend. We spent a day together just hanging out with everyone at a park. It was tough when the week ended, and I had to leave my family. I knew I was going to miss them.

When I returned home to Niagara Falls, I discovered that Grayson was sleeping with another girl who lived in the motel. My stepmother informed me that Grayson visited the girl's room multiple times while I was away. She had witnessed them kissing and holding hands, and they would disappear into her room. Grayson again explained himself away. He said that they had not slept together. I chose to believe and forgive him. We continued dating. The girl left the motel. Grayson fired my stepmother.

Grayson surprised me with a new Cocker Spaniel puppy. I named her CJ. Her coat was a blended white and cream, accentuated with long, silky fur. She was adorable, and I spent most of my time with her. I would take her for long walks around the motel. I fell for her hard and fast. Grayson exhibited signs of jealousy. He ruled that she could not sleep in our motel room. He made her stay in the motel room next to us. He did not like my attention being on the puppy. He appeared jealous and resentful of the love I had for the puppy.

Approximately a month later, CJ went missing. Grayson and I searched everywhere for her but could not find her. For weeks, I kept searching the area around the motel. I put up posters. I thought she had run away. I was consumed by grief, mourning her absence and shedding tears for days. About a year later, after my relationship ended with Grayson, I did uncover the heart-wrenching truth: he had given CJ away, allowing me to believe that she had run away.

The motel job ended. Grayson had been dishonest by failing to record the money received from room rentals. It was clear that he had been pocketing the cash for himself. Stealing and lying had become a recurring pattern for Grayson. Grayson took advantage of his friends and even strangers. In hindsight, this should have been a significant warning sign that I either didn't notice or chose to overlook entirely. The owner discovered that Grayson was stealing from him and fired us both.

Grayson had a mean streak. He was physically abusive and highly controlling. He also knew about my past. I had shared my secrets with him. He used this information to his advantage. He liked being the alpha of the relationship. I was quickly controlled and manipulated. I did not have a backbone. He would attack me if he did not like how I spoke to him or if I did something that he did not like. He beat on me. He choked me to the point of almost passing out. I would have to cover the bruises on my face with foundation many times. I remember wearing long sleeves or pants to cover up other areas of my body that were black and blue because of him. But I still stayed with him.

He would disappear regularly. I would come to find out that he was a womanizer and a liar. This was a constant throughout our relationship. He would lie to cover up the fact that he was cheating, and I would accept it and look the other way for some reason. I am unsure if I did not want to be alone. I had grown up with abuse, so I might have found I felt normal living in it.

After these abusive attacks, I would cry. I told him that it was extremely triggering for me because of my father. He would "sweet talk" me and apologize. He said he would do better. He reiterated that he loved me. I would end up staying. I remember thinking I could change and mould him into a nice guy. I was very naïve at this time in my life. I chose to see only his good qualities.

LOVE YOURSELF AND NOBODY ELSE

You can only find love

Once you love yourself

No one can teach you

Love should not hurt

But hurt can cause love

You can learn from hurt

But cannot learn about love

Love is a concept yet not understood

Probably never will be throughout your life

But always remember first to love yourself

And that's what love really is

Don't worry about if anybody loves you

Love yourself and ignore the few

Written on March 09, 1997

CHAPTER EIGHTEEN - EXPOSED

GRAYSON AND I DECIDED TO move to British Columbia for a fresh start. I was entirely on board with this plan because I missed my mother, brother, and sisters. This would have been a much harder decision for Grayson as he did not know my family and was leaving his family behind in Niagara Falls.

It was the end of summer in 1996. We flew out on an airplane. We moved in with my stepfather, mother, sisters, and little brother. They lived on Wellington Street in Port Coquitlam, BC. Grayson and I set up a bedroom in the basement. There were rules attached to being able to stay with my stepfather and mother. I had to enroll in school. I attended Terry Fox Secondary School. Grayson had to get a job. Grayson started looking for employment. We made friends quickly and had a social life. Colin (my future husband) was one of those friends. We got to know each other well. I also became close to Colin's girlfriend at the time.

At first, my sisters liked Grayson. My sisters, brother, Grayson, and I were hanging out in the basement of my mother's house, watching a movie together. My middle sister sat with us. She leaned her head against Grayson's leg. My stepfather came down and immediately got mad at my middle sister. He slapped her and told her to move. I found this quite odd, and Grayson did as well.

My mother must have perceived something was wrong with me. She had the skill of pulling information from you. We were in her bedroom having one of those mother/daughter talks. I started crying. I broke down and confided in her about the physical and sexual abuse throughout Grayson and my relationship. Grayson was asked to leave my mother's house. I made the difficult decision to end our relationship. He found temporary accommodation at a mutual friend's house while I continued to live with my mother.

My stepfather supposedly was furious after my mother had shared with him what Grayson had done to me. My stepfather found Grayson at the teen center and punched him in the face. My stepfather thought of himself as a white knight in shining armour. Separately, though, he told my middle sister that he had punched him because he caught Grayson staring through my middle sister's bedroom window. This did not happen. Grayson thought of my middle sister as a sister. I would come to learn that this was part of my stepfather's grooming with my middle sister.

A lot of my sister's friends appeared angry with my stepfather. I eventually figured out what was happening. Someone shared that my stepfather had done something inappropriate with one of my sister's friends. The rumour was that my stepfather went to her house when she was home alone and attempted to force himself on her. He asked her to have sex with him. I connected with her because I knew who she was. I told her that she was not the only one. I shared my experiences and my friend Marianne's experiences with her. I shared with other people as well.

No one from my family had told me what had occurred, and it felt like they were keeping it from me. My family was furious about me sharing my thoughts and feelings about my past experiences. I was told to keep quiet and stop spreading rumours. I was no longer keeping secrets like my father had taught me. I knew my stepfather was in the wrong. Again, I did not understand why my mother was staying with him.

I left my mother's house. Grayson and I got back together. He had gotten a tattoo on his chest with my name on it. He talked his way back into my good graces. I did say he was a smooth talker. We found an apartment together. We settled in.

There was a blizzard on December 29, 1996. It was catalogued as the "The Storm of the Century." Sixty-five centimetres of snow had fallen in 24 hours. The city virtually shut down. Highway 1 (the main highway) was shut down. The blowing snow made visibility terrible. We went out in that blizzard with our friends. I remember trudging through the snow to meet up with others at Lee Elementary School to go sledding. It was a blast. Grayson and I were used to the amount of snow because we were from Ontario. Ontario got a lot of snow.

A few weeks later, Grayson told me he missed Niagara Falls and wanted to go home. I remember that I wrestled with this decision. I had gained a little independence and my voice in BC. Our relationship dynamic had changed. I liked it and had deep connections with the friends we made. The internal struggle was real. I decided that I would move back with him. He bought two airline tickets. Colin, his girlfriend, and Greg drove us to the airport. There were tears. Grayson comforted me on the plane ride back to Niagara Falls.

TIME HAS PASSED...

Since I have thought of him last, a long time has passed.
I know I should not dare think about him and care.
He only played a small role in my life and then cut that part out with a knife.
He spit on me when I was down but then begged me to stay and not leave town.
I am not supposed to think of him, but I imagine breaking him limb from limb.
Am I a loser to think of this man like that, I wish I could rid myself of the rat.

He hurt me badly in mind, body, and soul, and sent me hurtling into a black hole.
A show was put on for me, it took him telling me to see.
He was unfaithful, dishonest, and hard to trust. He thought hurting me was always a must.
I caught him cheating and that was not fair. He had the gall to tell me that his unfaithfulness was rare.
Time passed on like it had been years and I feel that is why I can now shed my tears.
My feelings have now had a chance to come out. For him, why should I grumble and pout?

Time has passed. It is time to move on and forget about that cheat, fake, and con.
Time has passed, but I find myself still thinking of him. It is time for the curtain to close and the lights to dim.

Written September 03, 1997

CHAPTER NINETEEN - THE AFTERMATH

IN JANUARY 1997, GRAYSON AND I were back in Niagara Falls. We rented a rundown motel room. It had a bed, couch, and table with a separate washroom. It was one of those motel rooms where you would check for bedbugs. This period of my life was awful. I missed my family and friends in BC. Grayson was extremely angry with me about how the whole BC trip had gone. He was quick to get back to the man he missed. He started disappearing and sleeping with women. I think he was making up for lost time. He also started physically abusing me again. I found myself thinking deeply about the wrong decision I had made to return to Ontario with him.

In April 1997, he became angry because I had accused him of cheating again. This had become a prevalent argument between us again. We were in the motel room. I was sitting on the couch crying. He came over to the couch and grabbed me by the throat. He lifted me entirely off the sofa. I passed out. This was the last time he would put his hands on me in that way. My throat was bruised and swollen for days. It hurt to swallow. I told him I was afraid that one day he might kill me. He agreed that we should take a break. I moved out. I found a safe place at the YWCA on Culp Street. He remained at the motel.

Grayson and I continued to date on and off. I was having coffee with his uncle at the coffee shop near the motel. Grayson and I were supposed to meet for a date. He did not show up. I walked over to the motel and knocked on the door. A woman opened the door. She was naked. I spied Grayson lying in the bed – covered up with sheets. I asked her name. She stated it was Crystal. This caught me off guard because she had the same name as me. I told her my name was Crystal, and I was Grayson's girlfriend. I told her to leave because I wanted to speak with Grayson alone. She started to get dressed. Grayson told her to stop. He looked me dead in the eyes and told me that I was leaving. He said we were no longer dating. He told me I had ruined his life because of our trip to BC. He said he felt that I stripped him of his manhood. He said that he no longer wanted to see me. I left the motel crying. I was in shock. I could not believe I had left BC – my family and friends to return to this. I made my way back to the YWCA.

I remember running into two females on the bus around this time. They knew of Grayson. We got to talking; I pretended I knew of him. I did not share that we had just broken up and dated for the last year and a half. They spoke about an ex-girlfriend he had recently dated (little did they know it was me). They stated that she was dumb. They shared that he had cheated on her with forty or more different women. They joked about him having a notch in his bedpost for all the women he slept with. This is where I learned about CJ (my cocker spaniel) being given away. I believe one of the females had slept with him. They knew an unbelievable amount of information. I remember getting off that bus in shock. You would have thought that the information I learned would have given me the knowledge I needed to walk away from Grayson for good.

I spent the next four months living at the YWCA. This was housing for abused women. I turned 19 while living there. I had written in my journal that I did nothing for my birthday. I was struggling mentally. I missed Grayson. I would sit by the community phone booth at the YWCA and wait for him to call. It was pathetic. But he would reach out occasionally to connect, meet up, and have sex. I am unsure about why I did this. Looking back, I still cannot comprehend it.

My world was full of drama. I kept putting myself in dangerous situations. I would go to the bar often, as I loved to dance. My friend (Sherry) from YWCA and I went to the Croft (a local watering hole). We met a few players from a rugby team from London, England. We went back to their hotel to continue partying. The teammates were naked, jumping in the hotel pool. I thought these guys were wild and a lot of fun. Sherry made a connection with one of the players. His name was Steve. They planned to meet in Toronto the next weekend to see each other again before Steve returned to London.

Sherry asked me to keep her company and travel to Toronto. Sherry was nervous as she had just met Steve and did not know him well. I agreed to go for moral support. We arrived in Toronto. Steve was waiting for us at "The Bond Place Hotel." He brought us up to his room to drop off our bags. Tony (Steve's teammate) was sharing the hotel room with Steve. I had met him the prior weekend. We all went out to a pub called Freddies. It was a quiet atmosphere. There were not a lot of people in the pub. We started drinking. I could tell that Tony was interested in me. He kept leaning in and attempting to kiss me. I told him I was uninterested because I had just exited a serious relationship.

I drank too much. We went back up to the Hotel room to go to sleep. I realized then that Tony and I were sharing a bed. I was naïve. Tony continued making his advances, and I kept telling him I was uninterested. I finally fell asleep. I woke to Tony's hands under my shirt, attempting to loosen my bra. I asked him if he was hard of hearing. He seemed so determined. I remember thinking of the term "can't keep your hands to yourself." I turned on the hotel TV to watch a show. I believe Sherry could see that I was getting uncomfortable because she came and sat with me. Tony stopped.

I remember thinking we had one more day to go. I tried to ignore Tony as much as I could. It was a small hotel room. We went downstairs and got some drinks (Because this was a bright idea). We started drinking. Everything was fine until the evening. Sherry and Steve were in bed beside Tony and me, making out. This must have given Tony the signal. He started trying to make out with me. I told him nothing had changed, and I was still uninterested. I explained that I had just come out to support my friend, Sherry.

I got the overwhelming feeling I have had in the past. He was persistent. My mind went blank. I thought, here we go again. Maybe I should just let it happen, and then it will end. He was going for my belt buckle. I pushed him away and told him that I said no. I got up and left the hotel room. I needed some air. I decided I was going to leave. I returned, gathered my belongings, and told my friend, Sherry, I would catch a bus back to Niagara Falls. I called Grayson's uncle because I had no money for a ticket. He sent it to me. I left. This was the first time I was able to stop a man from taking advantage of me. I felt a new sense of power and immense relief. This incident did trigger old memories and feelings.

While at the YWCA, I spoke with my mother multiple times on the phone. I discovered that she, my sisters, and my brother were visiting Niagara Falls in August. I was excited. She also told me that my stepfather wanted to see me when he was in Toronto for work to discuss the logistics of my possible move back to BC. I agreed to meet him even though I did not want to.

In July 1997, I headed to Toronto to meet my stepfather. I remember being super nervous about the trip. I did not want him to make any advances on me. He took me to an Art Gallery. We went back to the hotel he was staying at. I felt uncomfortable and nervous. I remember looking at the hotel bed and thinking I was in a dangerous situation. I wrote in my journal that we had a six-hour talk about how I needed to change my life. It was one of his long-winded talks—the blah, blah, blah conversation. There were stipulations about me moving back to BC. I needed to make better decisions for my life. I had to get a job or finish school. He then took me out for dinner and to the bus depot. I went back home. I told my mother that the visit went well.

My welfare worker approved my purchase of a pair of new eyeglasses. I was so excited. This was the first pair that I would pick out on my own. I brought one of my friends from the YWCA to help me. I picked out a nice pair. Even now, I love to get new glasses. I think it gives me a brand-new look every time.

I had been in contact with my father on and off while I was staying at the YWCA. He was still using crack/cocaine. He brought my friend and I to my paternal family BBQ at Queenston Park. He had separated from my stepmother. I told him that I was thinking of moving back to BC. He seemed upset but did not have a say in my decision. I told him I would keep in touch. But we both knew I would not.

August 16, 1997, is the day my mother, sisters, and brother visited Niagara Falls. The day I moved out of the YWCA. My friends and I cried. We had shared great memories: epic moments, graveyard parties, long walks, and crazy adventures together. We shared in fights, tears, and laughs. I believe that we each contributed to a small healing piece as we all had faced challenges and abuses. We kept each other company through it. I would miss them but was happy to shut that door and leave.

At this point, I had not committed to the move to BC. I knew I would be going alone this time. I went back and forth in my thoughts, weighing the good and bad, who I would miss, who I would see when I got there, and where I stood a chance to have a better future. I contacted Grayson for the last time. He picked me up and drove me to a hidden spot. We said our final goodbye.

I have many journal entries surrounding this time in my life. My thoughts and emotions went back and forth like a ping-pong ball. I was not honest about the actual circumstances that were happening to me. For some reason, I felt I needed to be with Grayson no matter how much he hurt and betrayed me. My emotions and mood seemed to hinge on him, which is bizarre to my adult self.

I got on the Greyhound bus on August 29, 1997. My destination was BC. I was going to make the three-day trip on my own. I felt overwhelmed with both anticipation and sorrow. I knew I needed to leave Niagara Falls and Grayson if I was ever going to make something of myself. I spent the three days reminiscing and looking forward. I remember tears once we hit the Rockies because they were so breathtaking. A snippet from my journal read, "These mountains and scenery are perfect. I don't think I have seen anything more perfect other than this. They represent my strength and power to overcome life's challenges and risks. I love the inner feeling I get when I look at these giants."

STARTING OVER

Leaving behind a shattered dream,
I've sewn up my torn-up seam.
Embracing the best choice for me,
I'm finally breaking free, you see.

Journeying to some distant land,
Alone, without a guiding hand.
Driven by my inner fire,
Yearning for a fresh new desire.

Foolish I may appear to be,
Especially after being with thee.
I feel the beginnings of a new story now,
Without knowing what, who, when, or how.

I sense I'm finally in the light,
I did, however, have to put up a fight.
Please, no need for your pity,
I simply had to depart from that city.

Written August 29, 1997

CHAPTER TWENTY - DISCOVERING BC

I ARRIVED IN PORT COQUITLAM, BC, on September 1, 1997. My maternal aunt had also moved to BC to live with my mother. I attempted to live with my mother, stepfather, sisters, and brother. This lasted two months before I found myself leaving again. I felt the pressure of having to be good. The pressure of getting a job, attending school, and bettering myself was too much, and I cracked. I felt like the outcast of our family. I found myself dating again. I did not make the best choices in boys. The relationships were short-lived. I was smoking a lot of marijuana and drinking regularly. I was attempting to numb myself. I got into a big fight with my sisters because they told a school counsellor they were worried about me. I was pulled into the office to have a conversation about drugs and alcohol.

My stepfather and mother sat me down to talk to me. I told them that I could not help myself. I had gone through a lot of abuse. I did not know another way. My mother said, "Stop thinking about poor little Crystal and start thinking about others." I journaled about it. I wrote that I did not know how to do that because I was betrayed or let down whenever I trusted somebody else. I felt the pressure to prove myself to my family all the time. I could not change the ways I was living or thinking at the time. I was a lost and scared young woman.

I spent the next month couch-surfing and slept in a tent in "the magical forest." The magical forest was a park near Terry Fox Secondary. It was where the teens would sneak off to hide and smoke marijuana. In the center of the park was an old log with a Bus Stop sign that someone had stolen and put up. They changed the "bus" to read "bud." We all hang out there regularly, playing hacky sacks, hide and seek, stick wars, and sharing in storytelling. I did not stay there alone; my friends always slept in the tent with me. I felt like I was on a two-week camping trip.

I made friends quickly throughout my teenage years. Reading my journal entries, I noticed I threw myself into relationships—friends and boyfriends. After a day of meeting people, I would name them my best friends. I would write about how close they were to me and that I immediately trusted them. I doted on them and would be completely shocked when they let me down.

In November 1997, my friend Leslie spoke to her mother and asked her if I could live in their home. Her mother said yes. I was relieved. I had my own bedroom and felt safe. They were so kind to me. They gave me a sense of security when I needed it. To this day, I consider Leslie one of my absolute best friends. She has been a constant throughout my life and will continue to be. My relationship with my family was difficult at this time. I was not speaking to them. I wrote a letter to my mother expressing my feelings of hurt. We met up and had a long heart-to-heart. It was almost Christmas. We worked some things out and started to mend our relationship. This opened the door to repairing my relationship with my sisters as well.

My maternal aunt had told me that my stepfather had attempted to have sex with her and my other aunt. My aunt told me that they had kept it from my mother. I was sworn to secrecy.

I would not tell. I thought that news would have devastated my mother.

I felt very safe at Leslie's mother's house, but for some insane reason (another boy), I moved out on January 31, 1998, and moved in with a boyfriend and his parents. Suffice it to say that it did not last long. My boyfriend and I found ourselves residing at the Wild Duck Inn. Now, this was a real dive. When you turned on the lights, you saw cockroaches scattering.

During March break of 1998, my family went on an epic road trip to Disneyland. I said my goodbyes to my boyfriend at the time. The RV picked me up, and we made our way. I bonded with my little brother on this trip. We did fun activities in the RV. Disneyland was like nothing I had ever experienced. It was enormous and expansive. I went on as many rides as I could. I felt like I was a little kid. I met my idol, Tigger, and gave him a giant hug. Everywhere you looked, adults were dressed up as your favourite Disney characters. I had so much fun. I do not think there was one moment that I stopped smiling. We spent three days exploring the park. By the end, we were exhausted and ready to trek back home.

After leaving Disneyland, we went to Long Beach. I went swimming and collected some shells to bring home. At some point, my sisters and I had a conversation about my stepfather and his past sexual abuse. My aunts, Marianne, my sister's friend, and my experiences with my stepfather were brought to the surface. We were all secretly incredibly angry with him. On our way back home, we visited the Grand Canyon. It was a sight to see. My sisters and I did not want to hike down it, so we stayed at the RV. I think part of our reasoning was the previous conversation that we had shared. Our stepfather was not happy with us. He was very mad and felt we were being ungrateful.

On our next stop, we explored the stunning landscapes of Bryce Canyon National Park, which, in my opinion, surpassed the beauty of the Grand Canyon. Venturing into Bryce Canyon, we hiked to the enchanting Queen's Garden. The journey was spectacular with the captivating formations and the vibrant hues of red surrounding us.

I had journaled a lot about looking forward to going home and seeing my boyfriend. I had missed him terribly. After returning home, I quickly realized my boyfriend had left the Wild Duck Inn. His clothing and belongings were gone, and he was nowhere to be seen. I discovered he had hooked up with one of my best friends. He had slept with her, and they were now dating. This is a friend that I considered to be close. The whole experience was devasting. It was like my past was coming back to haunt me. It was another major letdown. I was not in a good headspace at the time.

Looking back, I see this betrayal would be a saving grace. I stayed single and swore off boys for four months (I know, a long time, right?). At the time, I felt like it was. I remember thinking I had been hurt for the last time. I spent time with my friends and family and went to raves, parties, camping trips, and bars. I had left the Wild Duck Inn and briefly moved to a few places. I did not spend much time at the places until I was on the move again.

On July 11, 1998, Colin and I confessed our love. He was one of my best friends then, the same Colin I mentioned throughout the book. I often called him my big brother. This was going to be tricky to navigate. How do you date your best friend without losing the relationship if it does not work out?

At first, our relationship was rocky – on and off. It was awkward and uncomfortable. I felt he was not the "usual guy" I would date. He was pleasant and kind to me. He did not scare me. I could not find many faults with him. He was not a "bad boy." We also did not want to lose the close friendship we had built before we started dating. He broke it off a few times until we officially decided to date on October 30, 1998. We had gone out to a Halloween Party, and he confessed that he did not want to be with anyone else but me. He was willing to lose our friendship if it did not work out. But it would be an epic love story if it did work out.

Around this time, I moved in with my friend Jessica and her son. Everything was moving along in the right direction. I felt I was happy. On November 27, 1998, I went to pick up my cheque as it was mailed to the old place I lived before moving in with Jessica. Abdul (I will name him) answered the door. He opened the door in a towel and a T-shirt. He stated the mail would not arrive until 3:30 pm. I would not have to wait long. I sat in the living room. He disappeared upstairs. I thought he was going to get dressed. He called me to come upstairs. I stood at the bottom of the stairs. He asked me if I would walk to the store and get him a pack of cigarettes. He held out a $20 bill and had some other paperwork in his hand.

I went up the stairs and told him I could do that. As I accepted his money, he grabbed my arm and pulled me into his bedroom towards his bed. He pushed me onto his bed and climbed on top of me. He attempted to kiss me, but I moved my head. I told him no and tried to get up. He pushed me down again and started to touch me inappropriately. During this, he must have taken off his towel. He was exposed, and he rubbed himself up against me. I told him if he did not let me go, I would flip out (not like I was not already). He kept repeating that he loved me and offered me $60 to sleep with him. I was appalled. I pushed and fought as hard as I could until I was free. I ran down the stairs and out of that house so fast.

Once outside, I noticed a girl standing up the street, getting into a cab. I ran towards her, yelling and asking her if I could get in. She must have seen that I was bewildered and scared because she let me. I was so terrified, but I had gotten away. In the cab with this stranger, I started bawling. The emotions of what had happened hit me all at once. I felt like I had been violated once again. I questioned myself about not seeing the signs. There were plenty of signs when I lived there. He would follow me and show up in the weirdest places. He always appeared on the bus when I was on my way home when I lived there. When he looked at me, I felt uncomfortable in my gut. He gave me the "no" feelings. I had spoken about him with my friends and Colin while I lived there. I asked the cab to pull over when I was far enough away. I got out and made my way home.

For weeks afterwards, I had reoccurring nightmares. It brought up a lot of my past sexual abuse, memories, and feelings. I told Colin what had happened. He comforted me. He also was angry that Abdul had done that to me. Colin and two of our close friends went to that house. He told Abdul that he should not have done that. He punched him and threw him around. He warned Abdul to never come near me again. Colin stood up for me. I think this was the first time anyone did something to protect me. I had not experienced this for almost twenty years of my life. I decided then that this was the man I was going to marry.

THE BATTLE BETWEEN PAST AND PRESENT

There was a time in my past,
Where the men in my life hurt me.
I hope this present time will last,
I will have to wait and see.

When I look into your eyes,
I can see that you are totally true.
But because of all the past lies,
It's hard to believe in you.

But when I feel your soft touch,
I feel totally secure and strong.
But because of the past pain, hurt, and such,
I sometimes believe that it is wrong.

But when your soft lips press to mine,
I feel the commitment that you give,
Yet, due to promises broken in time,
I'm not sure if it's worth trying to live.

But forget about the times in the past,
I totally trust, love and care about you.
I will make the present times last,
Make the commitment true.

Written on January 07, 1998

CHAPTER TWENTY-ONE –
THE FINAL STRAW

IN THE WARM SUMMER OF 1999, our maternal aunt from Niagara Falls, Ontario, visited. My mother organized a camping trip to the breathtaking Cultus Lake. Our group included my mother, sisters, brother, aunt, and my mother's friend. I visited on a few day trips while they were there.

My middle sister and I were hanging out on the beach alone. She stated that she was thinking about drowning herself or floating away. I asked her why she felt like that. She shared that she felt overwhelmed. I could sense that she needed to share her feelings. She started rambling off all the different memories of where my stepfather had sexually abused her over the years. There were so many incidents that seemed to hit her all at once. I sat and listened.

She first told me that he did not want her to go camping. He was attempting to keep her home with him. For some reason, he had not planned to go camping. He brought her out to the campground, and before he left, he continued to beg for her to go back to the house and drink with him alone, which made her feel repulsed and uneasy. This is what brought back the flooding memories of all the times he had sexually abused her. I thought this was mighty bold of him because my mother could have caught him or overheard him talking to my middle sister like that.

She had a murky memory of being at a restaurant with him alone. This must have been recent because she remembered drinking with him (she recently turned 19), but the rest had been blocked out. She stated that she had spent some time wondering what had happened because she could not remember the rest of that evening. To this day, she does not remember.

Both my sisters had graduated from high school a month earlier. My middle and little sisters were trying on their grad dresses in my middle sister's bedroom. She wanted to look perfect for her Prom. My little sister commented on my middle sister's small breast size. My middle sister became upset and started crying. This comment had hurt her feelings. This was quite common for my little sister. She seemed to compete with my middle sister all the time. My stepfather came into the bedroom. My little sister left. My stepfather told my middle sister that her breast size was perfect and then went on to touch them.

In December 1998, my mother, stepfather, and sisters went on a two-week trip to Hawaii. I remember being very jealous that they went without me. My middle sister shared that she remembered two incidents while in Hawaii. One was when they were at a beach. She was in the water when these giant waves started coming in. My stepfather had grabbed her under the water, pretending to save her from the waves, but he inappropriately touched her. She felt violated. She knew that he did it on purpose. She refused to go in the water for the rest of the day. She kept asking my little sister if she would join her because this would have made her feel more comfortable. She thought that if it were just my little sister and her, he would not come near her, and she could enjoy the water. My little sister would not because she was afraid of the enormous waves.

Her other memory was when my stepfather asked her to kayak with him. He told her that our mother did not want to go. My sister agreed to go. She liked kayaking. During the kayaking trip, he asked my middle sister to run away. She replied that she would miss her mother, brother, and sisters. She did not fully understand his comments and found it odd. He continued talking about the two of them travelling alone and that they would finally be able to be together the way he wanted them to. My middle sister then blocked out the rest of the kayaking ride. She remembers being off the rest of the trip and staying away from him because he would attempt to touch or talk to her inappropriately if she went near him. This made her feel highly uncomfortable and extremely nervous.

My mother told me my stepfather did not want to spend time with her during that Hawaiian trip. She felt she had done something wrong, and he was more invested in spending time with my middle sister. I think this was when my mother realized something more was happening.

My middle sister also shared about a different camping trip. She recalled lying beside our stepfather and mother in a tent. She could not remember when it was, but she felt it happened when she was young. In the middle of the night, my stepfather touched my middle sister inappropriately and mumbled some inappropriate comments. She blocked much of this memory out. She told my mother the following day, and the message she received was that my stepfather was dreaming and sometimes did that in his sleep.

When she had turned 16, my stepfather would take her out on driving lessons. During one of these lessons, he had her pull over on the side of the road and then proceeded to caress her breasts. After this, she refused to drive with him for a long time.

Around this time, he had snapped at her because she was leaning against Grayson's leg. Things were starting to become extremely clear to me. My stepfather had been abusing my middle sister for a long while.

This conversation also brought back memories for me. I remember him pulling us onto his lap and making us feel uncomfortable. Thinking back, what father figure pulls teenage girls onto their lap and attempts to cuddle them – not any. She also remembered so many times that he made inappropriate comments. He did the same thing to me. He made her feel uncomfortable by the way he stared, touched, or fondled her.

Back at the beach, my middle sister told me she had disclosed her memories to my maternal aunt the night before. Everybody had gone to bed; they were the only ones left by the campfire. After she shared what my stepfather had done. My aunt asked her why she had not said anything. My aunt mentioned my sister's age and said she should have known better. My middle sister explained to my aunt that she blocked most of it. She did not want to remember it. My Aunt asked my middle sister not to say anything to my mother until she returned to Ontario. My aunt was my middle sister's first attempt to seek help. She felt let down.

She had and still has blocked out a lot of the abuse. This was a survival skill she had learned when she was little. She often would go numb and forget things if she felt unprotected and not safe. The term for it is called disassociation. It is common for adults when they have been through the type of childhood trauma that we have endured. She honestly could not remember them. I reassured her that it was not her fault. My stepfather had been grooming her for years. He was the one in the wrong. He took advantage of the fact that she had come from past abuse.

My mother figured out what was going on later during that camping trip. My Aunt confirmed what she suspected. This was very overwhelming for my mother and sisters. My mother called my stepfather on the phone and told him that she knew what he had done to (my middle sister). She broke up with him and advised him to leave and immediately remove his belongings from the house. He was not to be there when they returned home. I am unsure of what his response was. My little sister freaked out and worried more about how she would pay for college, as my stepfather had promised her he would. My little sister did not support or empathize with my middle sister. I found this quite odd.

My middle sister felt that my mother and little sister did not support her initially after she disclosed my stepfather's abuse. My mother invited my stepfather for Christmas six months later. My middle sister felt like she was having a major anxiety attack and asked to go to the hospital before my stepfather was to arrive at the house. She begged them to take her. She just wanted to get away. She now realized that she was overwhelmed and anxiety-ridden over the fact that he was coming to the house, and she would have to see him. My little sister responded to my middle sister's reaction by telling her to stop pretending. She told her that it was not all about her. My little sister told my middle sister that she would not take her to the hospital. This was when my middle sister had an emotional breakdown from all the pent-up disappointments. She remembers losing her mind. She screamed at my mother and little sister and went to her bedroom.

My mother's message during this time was that she had invited my stepfather because of my little brother. My mother was struggling with accepting the fact that her husband had done this to my middle sister and also how she was going to make it work for my stepfather and little brother.

When I arrived, it was extremely awkward. My stepfather was acting so smug that I wanted to wipe the smirk off his face. I went straight to my middle sister's bedroom as she was not in the house's main area. She appeared extremely upset and felt extremely unsupported. She bawled her eyes out, and I sat with her most of the time. I let her vent her feelings of disappointment and anger. I did not want to be around my stepfather either. I hated him. I hated him because of what he had done to the family.

My stepfather's response to the reason he had sexually abused my middle sister left me stunned. He blamed her for not stopping his advances and felt my middle sister led him on. He thought that she wanted him to touch her inappropriately. He told my mother he accidentally fell in love with her. He also stated that if my middle sister had such a problem with his advances, why had she not told my mother? He almost appeared angry that his plan did not work out how he wanted it to. He did not feel like her stepfather and believed they could have had a future together. I found this so bizarre.

My mother briefly thought she could make it work between them but quickly realized it would be impossible. The real damage had been done. At first, she questioned his reasoning and was angry at my middle sister for not telling her. Now, she knows he was in the wrong. At the time, he was the grown man who took advantage of his daughter. My mother had to go through her own trials and tribulations. Her heart had been broken. She had to process how she initially reacted when she found out. She had to work through her part of the blame for continuously making excuses for him. She does not talk to my stepfather anymore.

MY SECRET PLACE

In the chamber within my heart, a secret place resides,
With each step leading down, there's no need for
rushing strides.
Down a stairway of marble stone, the descent does start,
Banisters adorned with ivy where white flowers are born in the
stem's heart.
 At the end of my long descent down is where I find I stand,
 Before me lies a door, the only key is in my hand.
 I cast a swift glance around, no soul in sight,
 Then open the door to my secret place as the time is right.
Upon shutting the door behind me, fireflies start to glow,
One by one, lighting up my secret place, my design begins
to flow.
In the middle of my space, there is a fountain I will see.
The sound of trickling water, a gentle melody, sets my
spirit free.
 In the fountain waters, an assortment of coloured fish swim
 and play,
 Lily pads are scattered here, frogs have found their way.
 Close to the fountain, an iron bench waits for me,
 Beneath a weeping willow, my favourite kind of tree.
Upon my seat, I settle in, listening to nature's psalm.
As I clear my mind of useless thoughts, bringing in the calm.
Looking around, I view fields of flowers, a colourful,
vibrant array.
Reflecting on the life I have lived in my safe, secret place, I stay.
 In my secret space, I confront the pain and abuse I
 have endured,

Reaching into my inner self, sending a feeling of peace assured.
Releasing raw emotions, finding safety in their sound,
Embracing the child I was, providing her with love I found.
After I have released all the pain that I hide,
I leave my space, locking the secret door with pride.
Up the stairwell, I climb with a new sense of grace,
Healing my soul and mind in my secret place.

Written by July 17, 2024

CHAPTER TWENTY-TWO – NEW HOPE

WE ARE GOING TO BACK up my story a little bit. In February of 1999, I found out I was six weeks pregnant. I called my mother first. She took me out for coffee. I was so frightened because I was young and did not have my life together like I imagined I would have when having a baby. I also called Colin's work. His co-worker broke the news to him by telling him he would be a father. Colin freaked out. He did not talk to me for a few days. Looking back, I could have done the reveal a bit more discreetly.

In April 1999, Colin and I decided to move in together and get ready for the new little one. His parents were not thrilled with us having a baby so young. This is when I started to get to know his family. He came from a strong family. They had immigrated to Canada from England. I had never met a family more put together than his family. Colin had two younger brothers who are now my brothers. Colin had grown up in a healthy, well-adjusted home. His parents would often push him to do better and work harder.

Our first place was a small basement suite. The owner lived above us. He was a short Italian man who was genuinely nice.

I celebrated my 21st birthday pregnant. I was on an emotional rollercoaster. I was going to be someone's mommy. I felt very strongly that being a mommy was an incredibly special job. I remember feeling the baby kick. A little one was growing inside my belly. I also was terrified and worried about the future – being a mother and a girlfriend. How would I do this when, until this point, all I experienced was the opposite of what I needed to know? I needed to know how to love, trust, and care for my new little one and my boyfriend, who would one day be my husband.

Colin worked hard. We bought all the baby furniture and clothing we thought we needed. Colin wanted to provide for his new little family. He was working two jobs at the time. He was also scared to become a father. He constantly thought of the future. He honestly did not think we were ready, but whether we were prepared or not, the baby was coming. We were both young and inexperienced with becoming parents.

Colin took a road trip to Prince George in September 1999. He drove one of his dear friends to a court hearing there. Prince George was ten hours away. I was very anxious and angry with him because my due date was October 10. I worried that he would not make it back in time for the birth. I found this to be very immature of him. He did make it back, though.

On October 03, around 7 pm, my contractions started. Colin slept while I went through the night with sporadic contractions. I woke him up at 6 am as it was time; my contractions were finally 5 minutes apart. We grabbed the hospital bag that we had packed. Colin drove me to the Royal Columbian Hospital in New Westminster. My mother and sisters met me there. My water had not yet broken, so the doctor broke it. I immediately was in hard labour. Multiple times, the nurses checked to see how far I was dilated. The process was slow. They told me at 5 pm that I was only 3 centimetres dilated and needed to be 10 centimetres. I decided I would take the Epidural. Colin went out for food at a restaurant nearby and let me sleep. An hour later, I was ready to push. My mother and Colin were in the room. My baby boy was born at 7:11 pm on October 04. He was 8.8 pounds and 21 ¼ inches long. I became a mother, and Colin became a father. He was a beautiful baby boy. We named him Reese Colin Morrison.

All my worries about whether I could love and care for this child went out the window. I spent the first night with him alone in the hospital. I gazed at his sleeping face. He was so precious. I held him bundled up tightly close to my heart and made him the promise that he would never experience the life that I had. Something changed in me that day. This new addition filled something inside of me that had never been before. My heart was immediately filled with feelings of compassion and empathy. I felt more like my life suddenly had meaning. He completed me. I was going to be the best Mother I could. I actually would do better than my best.

In December 1999, Colin and I discovered I was pregnant again. Colin knew before I did, and the test confirmed it. We were a bit overwhelmed. I did not know if I could raise two children. The choice was easy, though, after seeing what Reese had brought into our lives. Reese was almost three months old at the time. He was so aware of his surroundings. He knew who his mommy and daddy were. I spent time staring at him when he was asleep. He looked so tiny and innocent. He was so very dependent on us. I remember thinking that I did not know how anyone could harm their child. I knew my children needed love, understanding, patience, and care.

Colin was a massive support to me at this time in my life. He helped with Reese. He would bathe, feed, and even change his dirty diaper (while his shirt was up, covering his nose and mouth). I would catch Colin looking at Reese with such awe. He adored him just as much as me. We were good together. We kept each other in line while taking care of each other. We were growing into a true family together (something I had not experienced).

In June 2000, Colin, Reese, and I moved into an apartment building. It had more space than the little basement suite, and it was conveniently a block down the same road as where we had lived, which made the move easy. Reese finally had his own bedroom. It took him a little while to adjust, but he loved it. He was now crawling all over the place.

On September 08, 2000, I awoke at 6:00 am. I went to get out of bed when my water broke. There was a puddle on our bedroom floor. Colin had left for work already. I called my mother. I told her that my contractions were 5 minutes apart and needed a ride to the hospital. Reese was having a sleepover at Colin's parents' house (Reese's nana and granddad's) – the timing was advantageous. My mother came quickly and picked me up. I remember breathing through the contractions in her vehicle on the way to Royal Columbian in New Westminster.

I had called Colin. He was on his way to the hospital. He arrived shortly after we did. I was not allowed to have an Epidural with this labour as I was already 10 centimetres dilated. I remember thinking that this baby was coming way faster than my first. I was pushing by 11:50 am. Without the epidural, I remember each push. My baby girl was born at 12:08 pm. She weighed 8.3 pounds. We named her Kayla Dawn Morrison. My family was complete. I vowed to mould and shape my children the best I could to become good human beings. This learning experience gave me immense pleasure.

We brought her home. She was a sweet little thing. I was much more confident with her. I remember Colin gazing at her. I am sure having a little girl was a different experience for him. His whole family was so happy as she was the first girl born after they had a generation of boys. For Colin's father (Grandad), it was more than one generation of boys. Reese was usually gentle with her. I remember him creeping up to her bassinet and looking at us, saying, "Shhh!" and putting his little finger to his mouth. He adored his little sister. She was a perfect newborn. She slept a lot and did not cry much.

We celebrated Reese's first birthday a little less than a month later. He had his first taste of cake and loved it. He put his hands and face into it. He was a mess afterwards and needed a quick bath. He was a fast little guy, full of curiosity and very alert. He was climbing everything and quickly figuring out all the child locks. He danced to music—swaying back and forth and throwing his hands up in the air. He blabbed a lot in some foreign language that, for some reason, Colin and I understood. Nightly, we would read him a bedtime story. His favourite book was about a farm. Every time he saw Colin, he ran and jumped on him.

Colin was and is a great father. He helped out a lot, and his children looked at him with adoration. Colin and I taught and learned about each other. We had great battles. I realized that our ongoing arguments were of significant importance. I knew that he loved me, and I felt I could trust him with my whole life.

We moved out of the apartment and into a basement suite the following year. We were not long there before we settled into Colin's parents' basement suite on Apel Drive in Port Coquitlam. His parents rented it to us at a great price. It was perfect, and we appreciated their help. We celebrated Kayla's first birthday there. We had room for all the family. She was much more delicate about her first cake tasting. She did need a bath, though. She was now also walking. It was a much busier time for me. Reese would take her on adventures. He would break her free from her playpen. He could open locked doors just like I did.

One morning, I woke up to Kayla crying. I entered their bedroom – the window was open, but they were not there. Reese had climbed out and brought his little sister with him. There was snow on the ground. I ran outside to find Kayla and Reese in the snow with diapers on. I grabbed Kayla, and Reese followed me into the warm house. I warmed them both up.

Kayla was very cuddly and loving. She loved snuggles. She would kick Reese off my lap and take over. Reese did not mind, though, as he was not as cuddly. He wanted to always be on the go. He was into everything, whereas she was more watchful. She watched everyone like a hawk. He once broke eggs all over the living room floor. When I asked him what he was doing, he innocently said he played basketball. Colin caught him in the kitchen. He had poured all the spices out onto the counter. He had added Cheerios to them. He told his father he was making breakfast for him and his sister. It was tough to correct him. He was so innocent and thoughtful of his answers. I let my children get away with many things as I worked hard to break the cycle. Which I was remarkably successful at doing.

WHAT MOMMY SAID

He sleeps on his side
Mommy caresses his cheek
He pulls up his blankie to hide
Letting only one eye out to peek

My child is sleeping
In his warm crib, he lays
Dreaming of little birds cheeping
On the warm sunny days

One day, he will see the world
See all the challenges that lay ahead
And as he lay all warm and curled
He will understand what his mommy said.

Written on January 22, 2000

WHERE DID THE TIME GO

We've had so much fun
Watching you grow
You are already one
And you walk like a pro

From baby to tot
You're growing up fast
Time flies quicker than we thought
But the memories will always last

Reese, you make mom and dad proud
To have such a lovely son
We will scream it nice and loud
We love you a ton

You are a great little boy
Who has changed us for the best
Bringing laughter and joy
To our quaint little nest

Written on October 07, 2000

DAUGHTER'S GRACE

An unconditional love within me, I know,
While I watch my daughter gracefully grow.

I see within her the best pieces of me,
Strong and gentle, fearful, and free.

My daughter possesses the sweetest of souls,
Embracing many, multi-faceted roles.

She's an authentic and spirited artist,
A woman of grace, beauty, and the smartest.

I witness her make empathetic choices,
Being her own muse, sharing her melodic voices.

She cares with the entire might of her being,
For the ones she loves and those I am not seeing.

I will always stay devoted and be by her side,
As I watch my daughter grow with my heart's pride.

Written on July 29, 2024

CHAPTER TWENTY-THREE – LOVE CONQUERS ALL

ON AUGUST 31, 2002, COLIN and I vowed to spend the rest of our lives together. During the weeks leading up to our wedding, I was excited, nervous, and scared all at once. The plan was set: It would be a small celebration in our backyard. We had a potluck, where everyone invited would bring their favourite dish. We sent out invitations to our family and close friends. His parents had convinced us that we did not need a big fancy wedding. At first, we were both upset, but looking back, I realized it was the best decision, and I am glad we listened to them. It was intimate and genuinely represented who we were as a family. Both my children were with us. My son, the ring bearer, is in his little suit, and my daughter, the flower girl, is in a lavender dress.

I thought a lot about the man I was about to marry. In my journals, it was pretty clear that I was smitten. He was a wonderful man who gave me the stability and support I needed to grow. I felt comfortable and safe with him. Do not get me wrong; we both had our faults, and it was not perfect. But looking back, the imperfections were what made it special.

I remember getting ready in the morning. My sisters and close girlfriends were with me. I was more than prepared to walk down the aisle. The music we chose was perfect. My children had already made their entrance. My mother did me the honour of walking with me. I saw Colin standing there—tall, handsome, and nervous. We grabbed each other's hands.

The service went beautifully. I heard my daughter cry and say, "Mama." I beckoned to my mother to bring her up to me. I held her in my arms as my husband and I continued saying our vows, staring into each other's eyes. My son was sitting on the grass below, holding onto his father's leg. There was not much more that could have signified our life. It was perfect and unplanned. The commissioner said she pronounced us husband and wife and advised Colin he could kiss his bride. It was a passionate kiss. And I was now Crystal Morrison.

My marriage signifies the end of my secret life—my life before being Crystal Morrison.

ACCOMPLISHMENT

Holding my hands up to the sky,
A huge smile dawned on my face.
Come on, people, you need to try,
And strive for number one in life's race.

You can accomplish all your goals
And discover success within your setbacks.
Jump high over life's rivets and holes
Build up the needed supports and tracks.

Only you possess the key to your inner door
Have the power to unlock your dreams.
To live the life, you have been longing for
Overcoming life's obstacles and beams.

Confront your fears, one by one
You possess the power inside
To accomplish all that needs to be done.
To be your best self with no need to hide.

Written August 15, 1998

EPILOGUE

COLIN CONTINUES TO BE MY companion, friend, partner, husband, lover, and father. We have had our ups and downs. He has helped me heal, as I have felt safe with him. He has given me the independence and freedom to make my own choices throughout my life. He has never abused me. He has shown great patience through some of my more difficult areas of healing, the intimate parts. It has been a real challenge for him, as his love language is touch. We have raised some exceptional children who are perfect human beings.

Reese is 24 years old. He has grown into a real man. He struggles just like any young adult would in this society and world. He is compassionate and empathetic. At times, he has struggled. He is finding and making his own way. We have given him a great base to start with. I do not doubt that he will accomplish remarkable things.

Kayla is 23. I believe she has met her life partner. He is incredibly kind and supportive. He allows Kayla to be who she is. She has grown into an independent, well-adjusted woman. She is also maneuvering through life – learning and discovering. I do not doubt that they will find everything they seek together. I also believe that she will make an incredible mother.

We all live together in a big home in Abbotsford, BC, which Colin and I purchased together. I was my son's age when I got married. It has been 22 years. I feel my husband and I have created a calm and safe home. I have the support of great and endearing co-workers, family, and close friends. I have been able to maintain healthy relationships.

I have a vast support system and would like to take a moment to mention them. These are the people I genuinely trust and will always be a constant in my life: my husband, children, and daughter's boyfriend. My middle sister, mother, father-in-law, brothers and their wives, a niece, and nephews. My boss (mentor) and each one of my co-workers. My wellness coach. My close friends.

Last year, in October 2023, we lost my mother-in-law. This was a significant loss felt by all who were close to her. I relied on her a great deal. She showed me a different way to look at things. I will never be able to tell her how thankful I am for all the love, support, and lessons she brought into my life.

I have a career now. As mentioned, I am the Chief Operating Officer at a company that cares for youth. I love this career and have been doing it for 14 years. My middle sister works alongside me. She is the Safety Officer/Residential Coordinator. She just bought her first home. I feel that we have been mighty successful in breaking the cycle of abuse.

I have achieved many successes through hard work. I went back to college and graduated as valedictorian. I have bought and sold a few homes and a brand-new car. While I don't base my success solely on material possessions, I think it's important to mention them. I believe that with hard work and determination, anyone can break free from a cycle of abuse and make it. I am proud of the person I have become. I feel strong, independent, and accomplished. I am a role model to my children.

I do not talk to most of my paternal and maternal family. I feel that this was a piece that I had to leave behind. I had my last visit with them in Niagara Falls just after marriage. It was a challenging visit. The new person I was becoming clashed with the old person I left behind. I have chosen not to have relationships with my father, my stepfather, my little sister, my grandmother, certain aunts, and uncles.

Before writing this book, I felt I could not be vulnerable. However, through the writing process, I realized I had and have been vulnerable. I have healed over time. I am constantly healing. The wall I had built to protect me has crumbled. I realize I do not need it anymore. I knocked it down with each chapter I wrote and released. I have noticed a new intimacy growing with my partner, family, co-workers, and friends.

I have been asked about my pessimistic view of the world and others. I replied honestly that I came by it through my past experiences. I often find myself jumping to the most insane conclusions about people. It now takes a lot to earn my trust. Presently, I continue to work on my positive thinking. I have learned that everything has two truths: negative and positive. I now choose the positive most of the time.

I am grieving my little girl and the young woman I was through my writings. The sense of sadness for the time that they would never get back. The time to learn or experience a safe life without abuse and the things that were stolen from them. I gather them into my arms and console them each and every time that they reach out. I will continue to do this. I will continue my healing journey. I will work alongside my therapist when I know I need her.

I am honoured to share the story of my secret life, a burden I have carried for two decades. I wrote this narrative at age 46, intending to share my experiences with you, the reader. My ultimate goal is to make at least one person feel like they are not alone and that what happened to them happens to many. It is challenging for an individual to recognize their own trauma and understand that it was not their fault. I have found that the healing journey is the most difficult to walk.

It is important to acknowledge that abuse is prevalent in our society and does not discriminate based on any factors such as age, gender, or socioeconomic status. I feel it needs to be out in the open, not secret. I do not think any one person should have to deal with it alone. I hope that by sharing my secret life with you, you will be able to find the courage to share with others. I wish to inspire others to open up. Together as a society, I would love to see us improve and do better. I would love to see others learn that they, too, can break the cycle that has plagued us for centuries.

Printed in the USA
CPSIA information can be obtained
at www.ICGtesting.com
JSHW021135261124
PP13838200001B/1